Exploring
Galaxy Tab A

Kevin Wilson

www.elluminetpress.com

Exploring Galaxy Tab A

Publisher: Elluminet Press
Director: Kevin Wilson
Lead Editor: Steven Ashmore
Technical Reviewer: Mike Taylor, Robert Ashcroft
Copy Editors: Joanne Taylor, James Marsh
Proof Reader: Mike Taylor
Indexer: James Marsh
Cover Designer: Kevin Wilson

eBook versions and licenses are also available for most titles. Any source code or other supplementary materials referenced by the author in this text is available to readers at

www.elluminetpress.com/resources

For detailed information about how to locate your book's resources, go to

www.elluminetpress.com/resources

Table of Contents

About the Author

With over 15 years' experience in the computer industry, Kevin Wilson has made a career out of technology and showing others how to use it. After earning a master's degree in computer science, software engineering, and multimedia systems, Kevin has held various positions in the IT industry including graphic & web design, building & managing corporate networks, training, and IT support.

He currently serves as Elluminet Press Ltd's senior writer and director, he periodically teaches computer science at college in South Africa and serves as an IT trainer in England. His books have become a valuable resource among the students in England, South Africa and our partners in the United States.

Kevin's motto is clear: "If you can't explain something simply, then you haven't understood it well enough." To that end, he has created the Exploring Technology Series, in which he breaks down complex technological subjects into smaller, easy-to-follow steps that students and ordinary computer users can put into practice.

Acknowledgements

Thanks to all the staff at Luminescent Media & Elluminet Press for their passion, dedication and hard work in the preparation and production of this book.

To all my friends and family for their continued support and encouragement in all my writing projects.

To all my colleagues, students and testers who took the time to test procedures and offer feedback on the book

Finally thanks to you the reader for choosing this book. I hope it helps you to use your Galaxy Tablet with greater understanding.

Have fun!

Galaxy Tablets

The Galaxy Tab A Series is Samsung's line of mid-range tablets based on the Android Operating System for mobile devices.

There are two major Android lines available: the high end Tab S series and the mid range A series. There is also an 'active' series that comes with a hard shell protective case making it suitable for small children, travelling, and other heavy use.

In this guide, we'll concentrate on the Galaxy Tab A series.

Available Models

There are currently three lines of Samsung Galaxy A Tablets available on the market.

Galaxy Tab A Series

This is Samsung's mid range series of tablets and are usually well suited to email, web browsing, playing a few games and so on. They lack some of the features of the S series and are a bit slower with smaller screens.

There are three models currently on the market.

Tab A 10.1"

Tab A 10.5"

Tab A 8.0"

These models are almost the same, except for the screen size and a few minor differences.

For each model there is a WiFi only version and an LTE version. The LTE version allows you to add a SIM card and is useful if you use your tablet when you're out and about.

These tablets usually come with 32GB of on-board storage but can add more using a micro SD card.

You'll also find an 8MP rear camera and a 5MP front facing camera (2MP on the 8" model).

This series of tablets doesn't feature the S-Pen or a keyboard found on the S series. However, you can pair bluetooth keyboards with this tablet should you need to.

Android

Android is a mobile operating system primarily developed by Google, and is designed to run on smartphones and tablets.

An Operating System is a program that manages the device's hardware resources such as memory, processor and storage. The Operating System also provides a platform for you to run apps such as web browsers, maps, email, photos, games and so on.

Android is also known as open source, meaning the source code for the operating system is made available to developers and other manufacturers to use as they see fit. This is why android tablets and phones developed by different manufacturers look slightly different.

Google also bundle their proprietary apps with Android, so you'll be able to use Google Maps, Drive, Chrome, GMail, Photos, Play Music, and Google Play Store. You'll also find Google Docs word processor, Sheets spreadsheet, Slides and some other productivity apps.

Each major version of the android operating system has a dessert-based codename, and they appear in alphabetical order.

Android 1.5 Cupcake (mid-2009)
Android 1.6 Donut (late 2009)
Android 2.0 & 2.1 Eclair (late 2009)
Android 2.2 Froyo (mid-2010)
Android 2.3 Gingerbread (late 2010)
Android 3.x Honeycomb (early 2011)
Android 4.0 Ice Cream Sandwich (late 2011)
Android 4.1 to 4.3 Jelly Bean (mid-2012)
Android 4.4 KitKat (late 2013)
Android 5.x Lollipop (late 2014)
Android 6.0 Marshmallow (late 2015)
Android 7.x Nougat (2016)
Android 8.x Oreo (2017)
Android 9 Pie (2018)
Android 10 Q (2019)

The android user interface is a touch screen, meaning you can directly manipulate sliders, switches, buttons and icons on screen using your finger.

Android has a main screen called the home screen containing icons that represent apps.

Samsung created their own interface for their tablets and phones based on Android Pie called "One UI." One UI has all of the same Android features, while adding some additional tweaks.

Various icons and the Google search bar have been moved closer to the bottom of the screen so that they're easier to reach.

There is also a built-in dark mode for the system and Samsung's own apps, and the overall aesthetic has its own unique style.

Setting up Your Galaxy Tab

If you've just bought your new Galaxy Tab and taken it out the box, the process to set it up to use for the first time is very simple. You don't even have to connect it to your computer.

You'll need to charge your tablet, then run through the initial setup. This involves connecting to your WiFi, signing in with your Google Account, and setting up security.

You can also add your email and social media accounts.

Insert your SIM

Make sure your device is off before doing this. If you have the LTE model of the Galaxy Tab, you'll need to insert a SIM card from your network provider. Find the SIM card tray on the side of your tablet.

Push the end of a paper clip into the release hole until the tray pops loose. Pull out the tray.

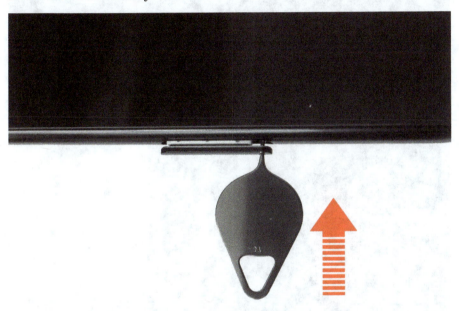

When you pull out the tray, you'll see two sections. One for a micro SD card and one for a nano SIM card. Note, you'll only see the SIM card section if you have the LTE version of the tablet. If you're using the WiFi only model, you wont see the SIM card section.

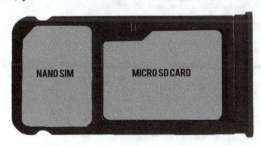

Chapter 2: Setting up Your Galaxy Tab

Insert the SIM card into the tray - it will only go one way. Slide the little tray back into your device, until it fits firmly into place against the side - it will only go one way up.

Charging your Battery

You can plug your Galaxy Tab directly into the charger to charge the battery, without having to go through a computer.

Plug one end of the USB cable into the charger, then plug the other end of the cable into the micro USB port on the bottom of your Galaxy Tablet.

Your battery will take a few hours to charge. Best practice is not to let your battery deplete completely, charge it up when you still have about 20% charge left.

Power Up

Once your Galaxy Tab battery is fully charged, press and hold the power button on the top right hand edge for a couple of seconds until you see the Samsung logo.

Shut Down

To completely shut down your Galaxy Tab, press and hold the power button for a few seconds, until you see the shut down prompt on your screen.

Tap 'power off' on the prompt to shut down your Galaxy Tab.

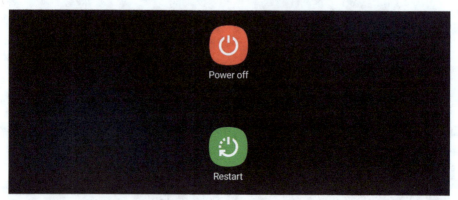

It's a good a idea to completely power down your Galaxy Tab from time to time to reset its resources - this can help when your Galaxy Tab seems to be running slower than usual. Most of the time your Galaxy Tab goes into sleep mode when in normal use.

Force Shutdown

Sometimes your Galaxy Tab can become unresponsive or freeze. When this happens you can force a shutdown.

Press and hold the Power button and the Volume button down at the same time for more than 7 seconds to restart it.

Your tablet will restart...

Once your tablet restarts, you'll need to enter your pin.

Upgrading Android

Make sure your Galaxy Tab is plugged into a power charger and that it is connected to your WiFi. Swipe downwards from the top edge of the screen, then tap the settings icon in the top right corner.

Scroll down the list, then tap 'software update'.

Tap 'download and install'

If there are any android updates, your tablet will download them now.

Allow your tablet to restart and install the app. This will take a few minutes to complete.

Initial Setup

When you start your Samsung Galaxy Tab for the first time, you'll need to run through the initial setup to configure your device to your personal account and settings.

Power on your tablet, and tap the 'lets go' icon in the middle of the screen.

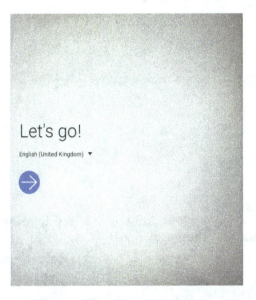

Tap 'i have read and agree to all the above'. Tap 'next' on the bottom right.

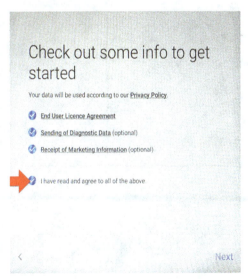

Tap 'skip this for now'. Tap 'next'.

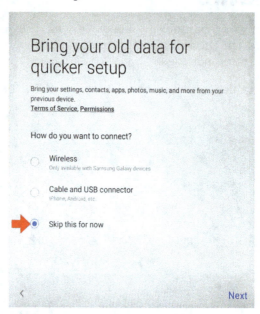

Choose your WiFi network and enter your WiFi password on the next screen. Tap 'connect', then tap 'next'.

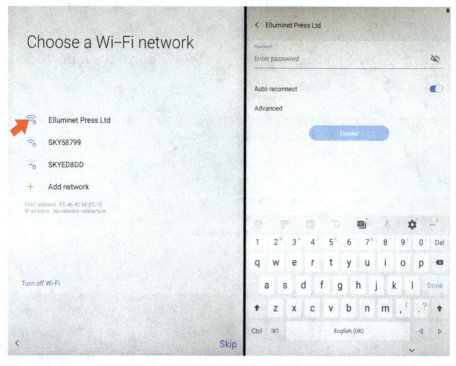

Sign in with your Google Account email address and password. Then click 'agree' on Google's terms and conditions.

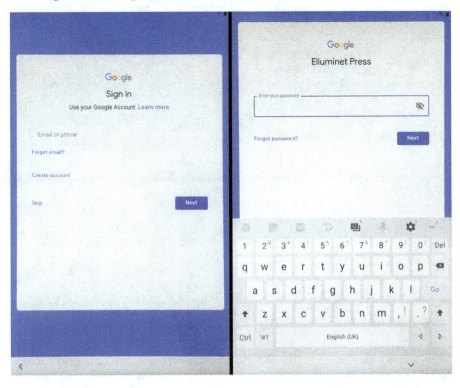

Adjust your date and time if they are incorrect, otherwise tap 'next'.

Set up access to your tablet. This is what you'll use to unlock your tablet when you turn it on or wake it from sleep mode. I usually use a PIN number but you can use a password if you want to.

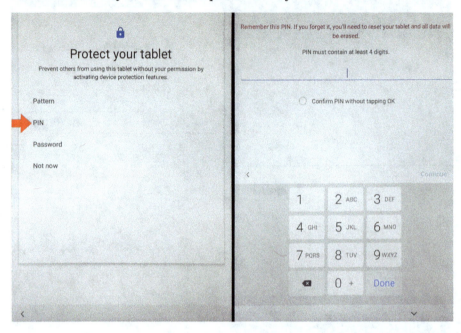

Scroll down and select the Google services you want and don't want. Read the on-screen descriptions as you go. Tap 'accept' on the bottom right when you're done.

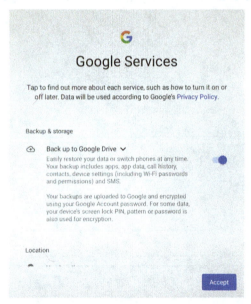

Next, select any additional apps you want. Scroll down and select 'ok' when you're finished.

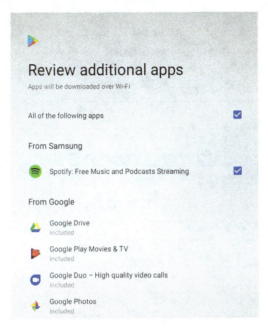

Add any recommended apps from Samsung if you want to use them. I tend to turn these off as I find the Google Apps are better. However, if you prefer the Samsung apps, then leave the tick boxes selected.

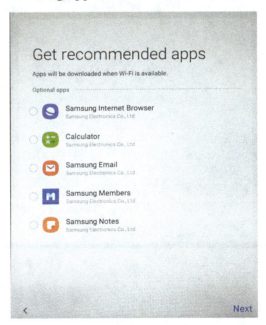

Chapter 2: Setting up Your Galaxy Tab

If you have a Samsung account, enter your Samsung email and password here, otherwise tap 'skip'.

Tap 'finish'.

Transfer Data from another Android

There are numerous ways to transfer your data from an old device to a new one. After testing, the best one I found was using an app called smart switch.

On an older Android device (Android 7 or earlier), or devices that aren't Samsung galaxy, you'll need to download the smart switch app from the Google Play Store. Open the Play Store on your old Android device and search for `smart switch`.

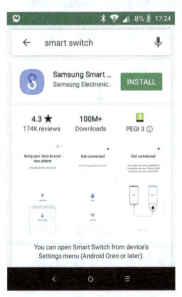

Tap 'install', then tap 'open', once installed.

27

On your Old Device

On your old device, swipe downwards from the top edge of the screen to open the notification panel, then tap the settings icon on the top right. Tap 'accounts and backup', then tap 'Smart Switch'.

If you do not have the app, download it from the Google Play Store.

Tap 'download' from the prompt at the bottom of the screen. Tap 'agree' on the next screen, then tap 'allow'. Tap 'allow' on all the permissions prompts.

Now, we want to send the data to our new device. So select 'send data' from the prompt.

Make sure your devices are placed side by side.

Select how you want to connect. In this case, select 'wireless'.

Now your old device is ready to connect.

Connecting your Devices

On your new device, you should get a prompt at the bottom of your screen.

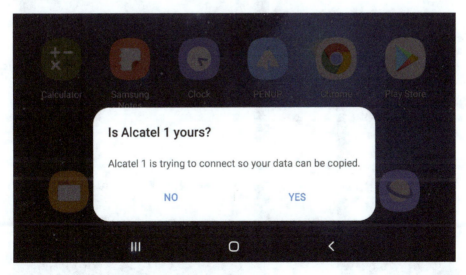

Tap 'yes' to accept the invitation.

Your devices will now attempt to connect to each other. This is usually automatic. If your devices don't connect, you'll need to enter a PIN code. Tap 'use pin' on the 'couldn't connect' prompt on your new device.

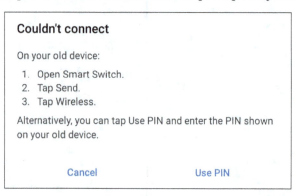

A PIN code will appear on your old device. Type this PIN code into your new device when prompted. Tap 'done', then 'connect'.

On your old device tap 'accept' from the invitation to connect. Then tap 'try again' on the 'cant connect' screen.

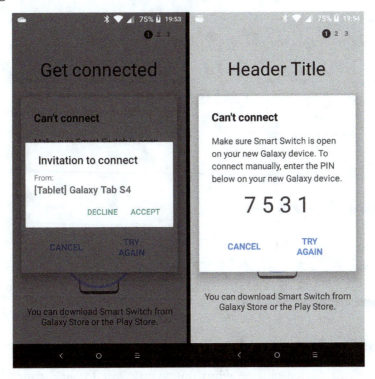

On your new device, tap 'wireless' from the 'get connected' page..

On the next page, tap 'receive data' (we're receiving from the old device).

Now, on your new device, you should see 'connected to…' at the top of your screen in big bold text.

Transferring your Data

On your old device choose what data you want to send over to your new device. Tap on the icons to select.

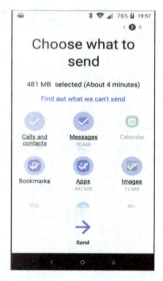

Tap 'send'. Your data will transfer. This will take a few minutes.

Transfer Data from an iPhone/iPad

After testing, the best way to transfer your data from and iPhone to and Android was to first back up your iPhone to your iCloud account, then on your new device, use and app called smart switch.

On your iPhone/iPad

First back up all your data to your iCloud account. To do this, open your settings app, tap your

Make sure 'iCloud Backup' is turned on, then tap 'back up now'

Give your data a few minutes to back up to your iCloud.

On your new device

Swipe downwards from the top edge of the screen to open the notification panel, then tap the settings icon on the top right. From the settings app, tap 'accounts and backup', then tap 'Smart Switch'.

If you do not have the app, download it from the Google Play Store.

Tap 'download' from the prompt at the bottom of the screen. Tap 'agree' on the next screen, then tap 'allow'. Tap 'allow' on all the permissions prompts.

Now, we want to receive data from an iCloud account. So, tap 'receive data'. From the next screen, select 'wireless', then select 'iphone/ipad'

Sign in with your iCloud Apple ID email address and password.

Enter your verification sent to your iPhone if prompted.

Allow your tablet to scan your iCloud for your data, this will take a few minutes. Choose what data you want to import - tap on the icons to select.

Tap 'import' at the bottom of the screen. This should bring over the data you selected.

This will take a while, depending on how much data you have.

Setting up Email Accounts

You can add all your email accounts to the GMail app on your tablet. To do this, open the GMail app, swipe downwards from the middle of the home screen to reveal all your apps.

You'll find the GMail app in the 'Google' folder. Tap 'Google'.

Select 'GMail' from the Google apps folder.

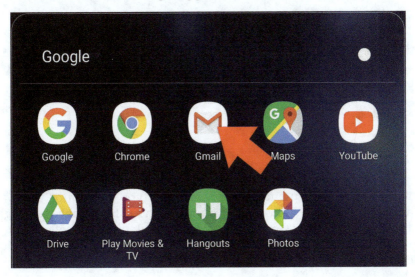

Once the GMail app opens, tap the hamburger icon on the top left to open the side panel. Then tap 'settings' on the bottom left.

Tap 'add account'.

Now, from the 'set up email' list, select the type of account you want to add. If you have a Yahoo account, tap 'yahoo'. If you have a Google/GMail account, tap 'Google'. For a Hotmail or Microsoft Account, tap 'Outlook, Hotmail and Live'. In this example I am going to add a Microsoft Account. So I'd tap on 'outlook, Hotmail and live'.

In the box that appears, enter your account email address, tap 'next', then your password. Tap 'next'

Tap 'next' on the 'account options' screen.

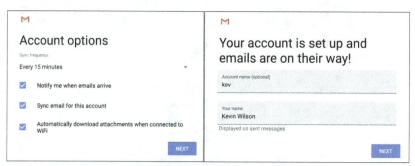

Tap 'next' on the following screen.

Add Social Media Accounts

You can add your Facebook and Twitter accounts to your Galaxy Tab. The easiest way to do this is to go to the Play Store and download the app for Facebook, Instagram, Twitter, and any other social media app you use.

First, open the Google Play app. To do this, swipe downwards from the middle of the screen to reveal all your apps.

Tap 'Google Play'.

Search for each of the social media apps you want to use. In this example, I'm going to install Facebook. Type 'facebook' into the search field at the top of the screen.

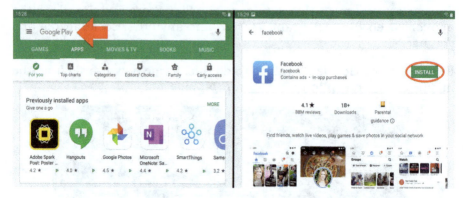

Once installed, tap 'open' on the top right of the Play Store. Then enter your Facebook username and password to sign in.

You'll find the Facebook app icon on your home screen.

Do the same with each of the other social media apps you want to use. Just search for the app names in the Play Store, as shown above.

Change your Wallpaper

You can set a photograph as a background on your lock screen and home screen.

Using an Image Taken with your Camera App

To use an image you've taken with your on board camera, tap and hold an empty area of the screen.

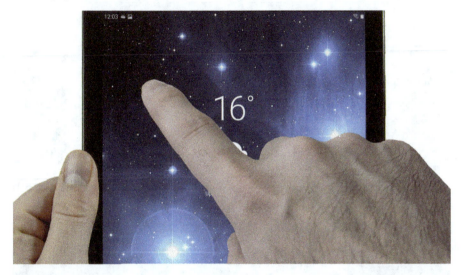

Tap 'wallpapers' on the bottom of the screen.

Tap 'from gallery'. This is where your galaxy tab saves all the photos you've taken with your on board camera.

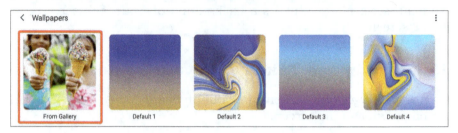

Select a photo.

You can apply the wallpaper to the Home screen, Lock screen, or both the Home and Lock screens.

Tap and slide the image to fit it onto the screen previews shown below.

Tap 'set as wallpaper'.

Using an Image from Google Photos

To use a photo from Google Photos, first you'll need to open the Google Photos app, and download the photo to your tablet. To do this, open the Google Photos app from your home screen.

Tap the photo you want.

Tap the three dots icon on the top right of the screen and tap 'save to device'.

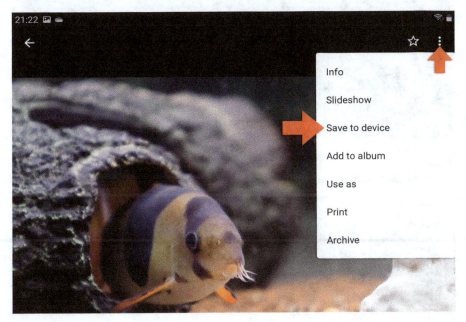

Chapter 2: Setting up Your Galaxy Tab

Tap and hold an empty area of the screen.

Tap 'wallpapers' on the bottom of the screen.

Tap 'from gallery'. This is where your galaxy tab saves all the photos you've taken with your on board camera.

Select a photo.

You can apply the wallpaper to the Home screen, Lock screen, or both the Home and Lock screens.

Tap and slide the image to fit it onto the screen previews shown below.

Tap 'set as wallpaper'.

Pairing Bluetooth Devices

You can pair bluetooth keyboards, headphones, and bluetooth capable hardware in some cars.

To pair a device, first put the device into pairing mode. You'll need to refer to the device's instructions to find specific details on how to do this. On most devices, press and hold the pairing button until the status light starts flashing. This means the device is ready to be paired with your Galaxy Tab.

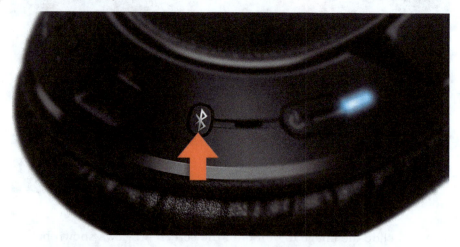

On your tablet, swipe down from the top edge of the screen.

Tap the settings icon on the top right

Tap 'connections', then 'bluetooth'. Tap the toggle switch on the right hand side to turn bluetooth on.

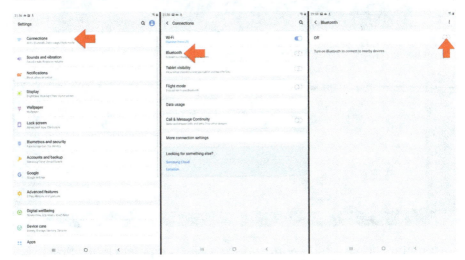

Your tablet will start to scan for nearby bluetooth devices. The devices will be listed under 'available devices'

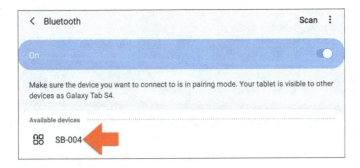

Tap on the device name to pair it with your tablet.

47

Adding Printers

Most modern printers will support cloud printing and are cloud-ready printers.

First, make sure your printer is powered on and connected to your WiFi.

On your tablet, swipe downwards from the top edge of the screen to open the notification panel.

Tap the settings icon on the top right.

Tap 'connections', then 'more connection settings', then 'printing'. Tap 'Default Print Service'. Make sure the toggle switch at the top is set to 'on'. Your tablet will scan the network for available and compatible printers.

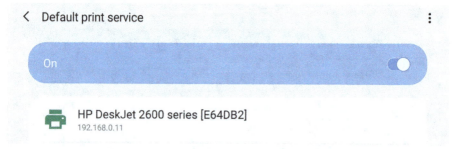

The default print service works with most modern WiFi printers.

If the default print service doesn't find your printer, or your printer is an older model, you can install the plugin for your printer. To do this, open the settings app, then select 'connections'. Tap 'more connections', then tap 'printing'. From the 'printing' screen, tap 'download plugin'

Select the plugin for your brand of printer... Use 'HP Print Services Plugin' for HP printers, 'Canon Print Services' for Canon printers, , 'Epson Print Enabler for Epson printers, and so on.

If in doubt you can use the 'Samsung Print Service Plugin' as it not only supports Samsung printers, but a variety of other brands too.

Connecting to a PC

Your Galaxy Tab Micro USB cable plugs into the port on the bottom of your tablet.

Plug the other end of the USB cable into a USB port on your PC or Mac.

This will allow you to copy music, photos, and documents onto your tablet directly from your computer

On your tablet, tap 'allow' on the data access prompt at the bottom of the screen.

Then on your computer, open file explorer

Select 'this pc' from the panel on the left hand side, then select 'galaxy tab A'

You'll see some folders. Copy music into the music folder, movies into the movies folder, pictures into the pictures folder, and documents into the documents folder.

Any photos or videos you've taken with the tablet's camera you'll find in the DCIM folder

Connecting to the Internet

With a Galaxy Tab, you can connect to the internet two ways: one is using WiFi and the other is using an LTE cellular connection if you've inserted a SIM card.

WiFi

On your tablet, swipe downwards from the top edge of the screen to open the notification panel.

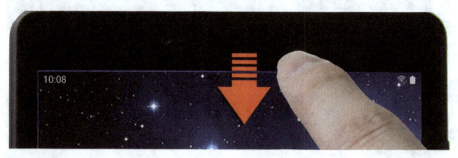

Tap the settings icon on the top right.

From the settings app, tap 'connections'.

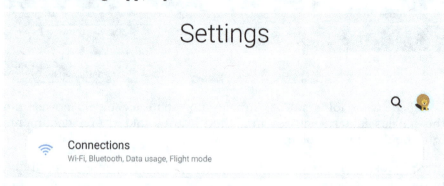

Tap on WiFi, make sure the blue switch is turned on.

Select your WiFi network name. The network name is sometimes called an SSID.

Enter your WiFi password then tap 'connect'.

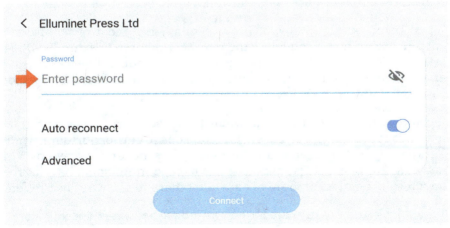

For your home WiFi, the network key or password, is usually printed on the back of your router.

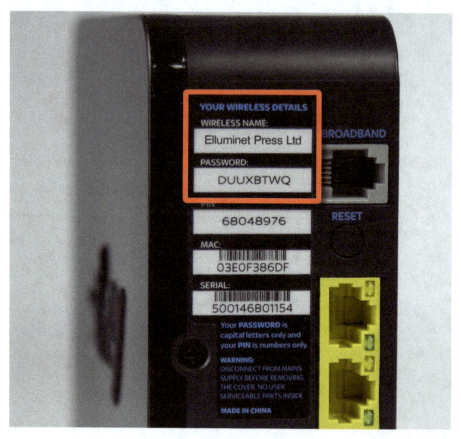

Use the same procedure if you are on a public hotspot such as in a cafe, library, hotel, airport and so on. You'll need to find the network key if they have one. Some are open networks and you can just connect.

When using public hotspots, keep in mind that most of them don't encrypt the data you send over the internet and aren't secure. So don't start checking your online banking account or shop online while using an unsecured connection, as anyone who is on the public WiFi hotspot can potentially gain access to anything you do.

If you're really concerned about security or use your devices on public hotspots for work, then you should consider a VPN or Virtual Private Network. A VPN encrypts all the data you send and receive over a network. There are a few good ones to choose from, some have a free option with a limited amount of data and others you pay a subscription.

Take a look at www.tunnelbear.com, windscribe.com & speedify.com

Mobile & LTE

After you have installed a SIM card and powered on your tablet, you will automatically connect to your mobile data service. You'll see an icon on the right hand side of your status bar on the top of the screen

To control your tablet's access to mobile data networks, open your settings, tap connections, then select 'mobile networks'.

Here you can turn mobile data on or off. To do this tap 'mobile data' to turn on or off.

Ideally when you're at home or in a WiFi hotspot, your tablet will automatically use the WiFi, but when you're out somewhere where WiFi isn't available, your tablet will select the mobile data instead.

Getting Around Your Galaxy Tab

Galaxy Tablets have touch screens and you navigate around the system using your finger to tap on objects on the screen. This could be an icon, and image, text field, and so on.

In this section we'll take a look at navigating around the interface, where to find things and how to get started.

For this section, have a look at the video demos. Open your web browser and navigate to the following website:

www.elluminetpress.com/galaxynava

Tablet Anatomy

Lets take a look around the Galaxy Tab A. Along the top edge of the screen you'll find the front facing camera.

Along the top edge, you'll find your 3.5mm headphone jack

Along the bottom edge, you'll find another two speakers, one on either side. In the middle is the Micro USB dock connector for you to connect the USB cable to a charger or computer.

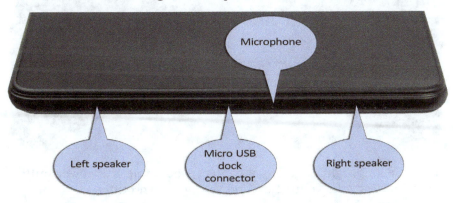

Along the long top left edge of your tablet, you'll see find the micro SD and SIM card tray.

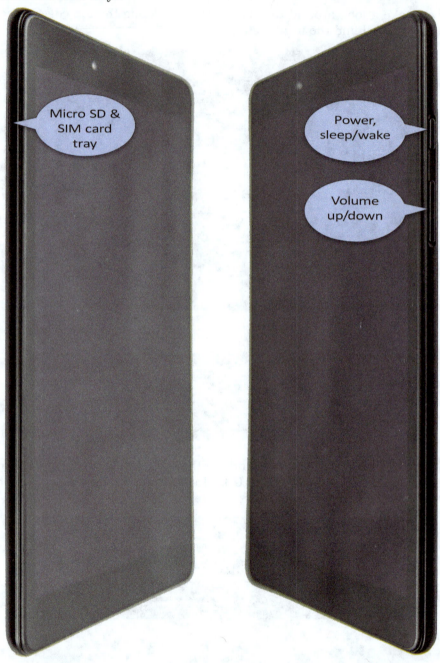

Along the long right edge of your tablet, you'll find the power button, and below that, the volume up and volume down buttons.

The Home Screen

When you sign into your tablet you will see the home screen. Lets take a closer look. Along the top of the home screen there is a status bar that displays current networks (cellular or wifi), current time, services such as bluetooth and battery life. In the middle of the screen you can add various widgets such as Google Search, Weather, Notes, or Maps, along with various icons for apps that you use.

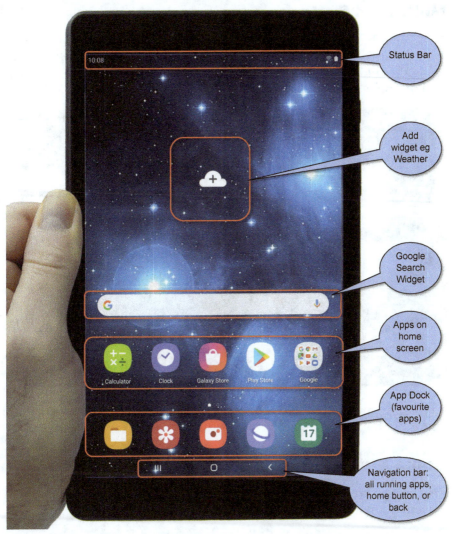

At the bottom, you'll find the app dock, this is where you can pin your most used apps (or favourite apps).

At the very bottom of the screen, you'll see the navigation bar.

Navigation Bar

On the navigation bar, you'll find three buttons: multi task, home, and back.

Multi-task Button

Also sometimes called the 'recents' button, shows all the apps that are currently running on your tablet. Preview thumbnails will appear along the middle of the screen. Tap on a thumbnail preview to switch to that app, as shown below left.

To close an app, swipe upwards over the thumbnail preview, as shown above right.

Home Button

Next is the home button, press this button to return to your home screen at any time from any app.

Back Button

The last icon on the navigation bar is the back button. Use this button to go back to the previous screen you were using.

Touch Gestures

Gestures, sometimes called multi-touch gestures, are what you'll use to interact with the touch screen on your tablet.

All it takes is the touch of a finger to use your favourite apps, navigate the web, and access all the things you need.

Tap

Tap your index finger on an icon, or to select something on the screen. For example, you can tap on an icon on the home screen to start an app.

You can also tap and hold your finger on the screen to access other options that might be available (this is like right-clicking the mouse on your computer).

Drag

Tap on an object on the screen, then without lifting your finger off the glass, run your finger across to drag up and down, left or right, or any other direction on the screen. You can drag icons, files, photos and so on.

Scroll

Tap and drag your finger up and down the glass without lifting your finger off the surface of your tablet. You can scroll up and down a web page, document or list of icons in this way.

You can also swipe your finger upward or downward to scroll faster.

Pinch & Spread

Hold your index finger and thumb on the area you want to zoom in or out on. Pinch the screen to zoom out and spread to zoom in.

Pinch is shown in the illustration above, with the small red arrows, spread is shown with the large red arrows.

Swipe

This allows you to flip through photos, pages in an e-book, pages on the home screen. You swipe the screen as if you were striking a match.

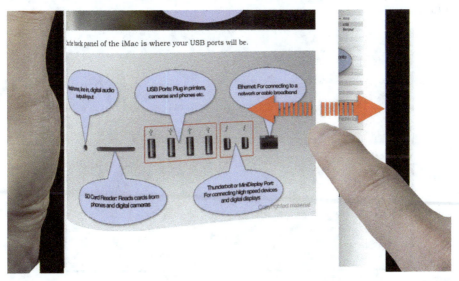

Notification Panel

Swipe downwards from the top edge of the screen to reveal the notification panel.

The notification panel will slide down from the top edge of the screen. Here you can see notifications from your various apps, as well as adjust WiFi settings, battery, orientation lock, bluetooth and more settings.

Underneath these controls, you'll see notifications from different apps. These could be system messages, reminders, or email messages.

To reveal the full panel, drag the small handle downwards on the bottom of the icon panel just above the notifications list, as shown below.

Lets take a closer look at the full notification panel. I've split the panel into different sections so we can see what each icon does. On the top right you'll see three small icons...

The first row of icons...

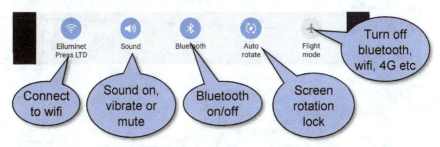

The second row of icons...

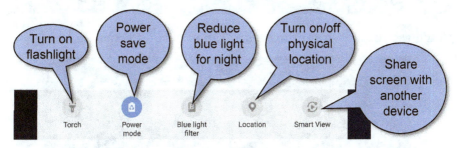

Along the bottom of the panel...

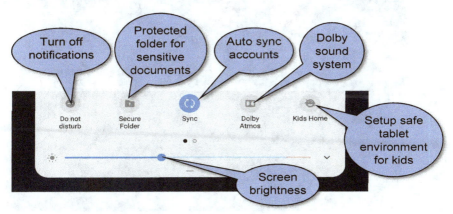

Reveal All Apps

To reveal all the apps on your tablet, swipe downwards from the middle of the screen.

You'll see the app drawer open up. Tap any icon to open an app.

App Dock

You'll find the App Dock along the bottom of your home screen - circled below in red.

This is where you can add your most used apps. To add an app, tap and drag an icon to the dock. A space will appear automatically on the dock for the app's icon.

You can drag icons from the home screen, or the all apps drawer - just tap and drag the icon to the bottom of the screen until the dock appears.

To remove an icon from the dock, tap and drag the icon onto another part of the screen.

Arranging Icons

You can move apps on your home screen. To do this, tap and hold your finger on an app icon, then without lifting your finger off the glass, drag the icon in to position on the screen.

If you have a lot of apps installed on your tablet, you might have more than one page of icons. To get to these icons, you swipe your finger left or right across the screen. If you want to move an icon to another page, tap and hold your finger on the app, then drag it to the edge of the screen. You'll see the page flick over.

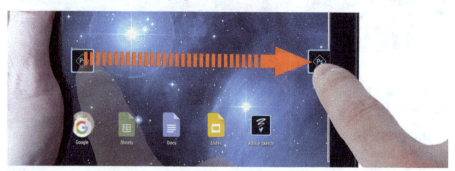

You can also drag icons off the all icons drawer. To do this, first swipe downwards from the centre of the screen to reveal 'all apps' drawer.

From the 'all apps' drawer, tap and drag the app icon you want, to the bottom of the screen. Release your finger when the screen changes.

The app will attach itself to the dock along the bottom of the screen.

To move it to any other part of the home screen, just tap and drag it off the dock into position.

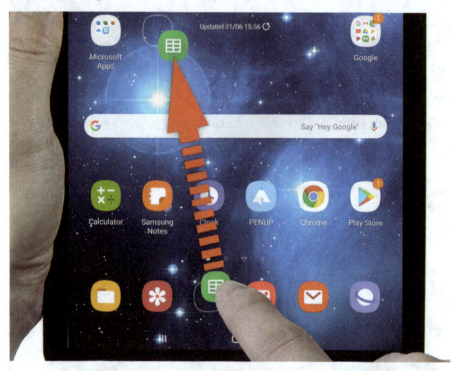

To remove an icon from the home screen or dock, tap and hold your finger on the icon. From the popup menu select 'remove from home'.

Google Assistant

Like Amazon's Alexa, Microsoft's Cortana, and Apple's Siri, Google Assistant is your voice activated personal assistant on Android devices.

To activate Google Assistant, hold down the home button for a couple of seconds.

You'll also find Google Assistant on the Google Search Bar. On the right hand side, you'll see a small microphone icon - tap this to activate Google Assistant.

Google Assistant will open up and start 'listening'. Now tell her what you want... Try "Find me somewhere to eat..." or "Tell me a joke..."

Google find the results for you.

You can also set reminders or appointments. Try this: "Hey Google, remind me, production team meeting tomorrow at 3pm."

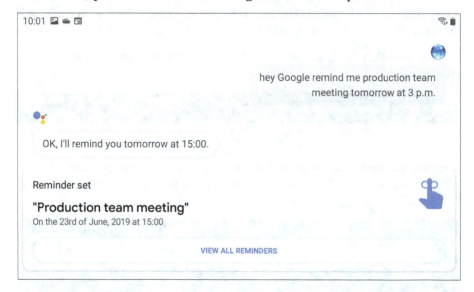

Google will add a reminder for you. To see any reminders, just ask Google. Try "show me reminders for tomorrow.", or "show me reminders for today".

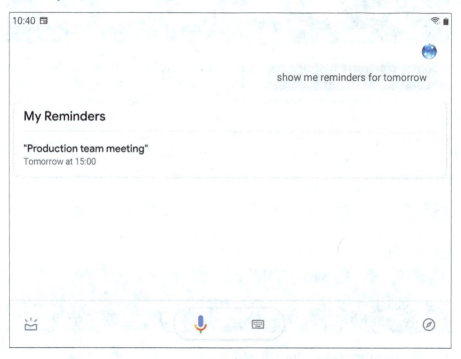

On Screen Keyboard

The on-screen keyboard appears whenever you tap inside a text field such as Chrome's Google Search, or open a document in Google Docs, a message in email app or your instant messaging app.

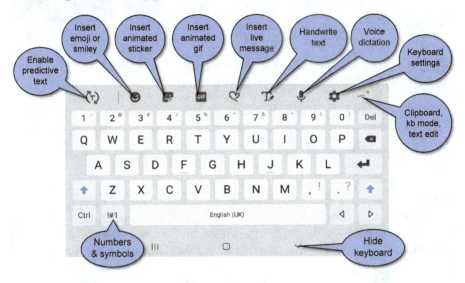

Tap on the keys to type in the normal way. Tap '!#1' on the bottom left to enter symbols such as $, %, ^, &, £ or numbers.

Along the top of the on-screen keyboard you'll see some icons.

The first one enables predictive text, where your tablet will try to predict the words you're going to use allowing you to select them rather than typing them in.

73

The next three icons allow you to add, emojis, stickers, and animated gifs. Just select the icon from the icon bar along the top of the keyboard

Then select an emoji, sticker or gif. Tap the little keyboard icon on the bottom left to return to the keyboard.

The next icon is the handwriting recognition feature.

You can use your finger to handwrite words instead of typing them in. For example, I'm going to handwrite a Google search into Chrome. Tap in the search field at the top of Google Chrome, them from the on screen keyboard select the handwriting recognition feature icon.

Your tablet will convert your handwritten text into type, and insert it into the search field for you.

Voice Dictation

You can use voice dictation to enter text or even dictate documents in Google Docs. To activate voice dictation, bring up the on screen keyboard. Tap inside a text field or document.

Along the top of the on screen keyboard, you'll see a list of icons. Tap on the microphone icon to start dictation mode.

On the bottom of the screen you'll see a dark green mic icon. You can now dictate your text to be entered into your document or text field.

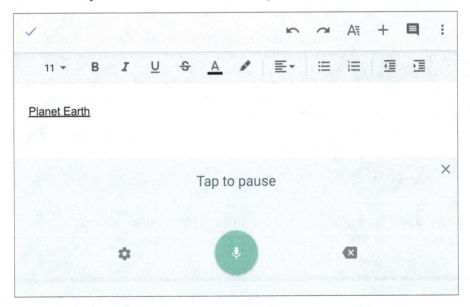

Tap the mic icon to pause if you need to. Tap the backspace icon next to mic icon on the right to delete a word.

Internet, Email and Communication

Your tablet has numerous features that allow you to browse the web, send and receive emails, share pictures with friends, store addresses & contacts, as well as have video chat conversations with friends & family.

To do this, Google have developed some built in app such as Chrome for web browsing, Gmail for email and Hangouts for video chat.

You also have Apps for social media, and an address book to keep track of contacts addresses and details.

For this section, have a look at the video demos. Open your web browser and navigate to the following website:

www.elluminetpress.com/galaxyacomms

Using Chrome

Chrome is a web browser developed by Google and usually comes already installed on your tablet. You'll find it in your apps. Swipe downwards from the middle of the screen to reveal all your apps. If Chrome isn't there, you should find it in a folder called 'Google'.

To make Chrome more accessible, tap and hold your finger on the Chrome icon, then select 'add to home'. This will add the Chrome icon to your home screen, so you can launch the browser without going through the 'all apps' screen.

Chapter 4: Internet, Email & Communication

Lets take a look at Chrome's default start page (or home page).

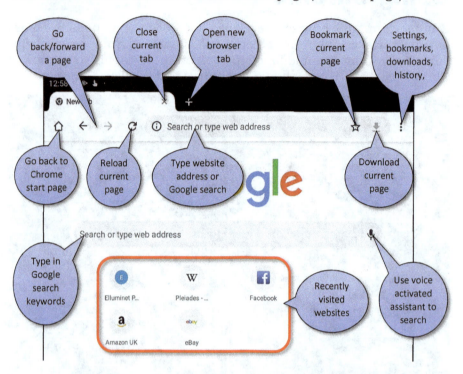

On the top right of the screen, you'll see a 3 dots icon. From this menu, you can open a new browser tab, view bookmarks, browsing history, downloads, desktop/mobile versions of a website, and adjust settings.

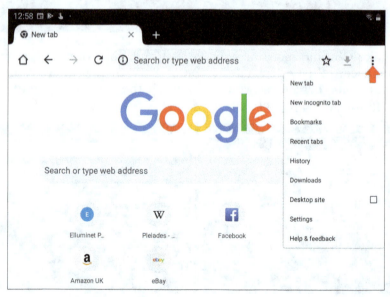

Searching the Web

Tap on the 'search or type web address' field at the top of the screen.

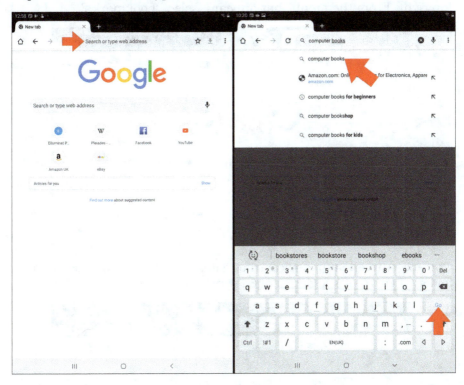

Using the on screen keyboard, type in the name of what you're looking for. In this example, I am searching for computer books. Notice as you type in, Google comes up suggested searches. You can tap on one of these to search for it, otherwise tap 'go' on the right of the keyboard to start your search. Google will return a list of websites matching the search. You can also type in the address of a website if you know it.

Bookmarking Websites

To bookmark the website you're currently looking at, click the 'star' icon on the top right.

Return to a Bookmarked Website

To go back to sites you have bookmarked, click the '3 dots' icon on the top right. From the menu that appears, select 'bookmarks'.

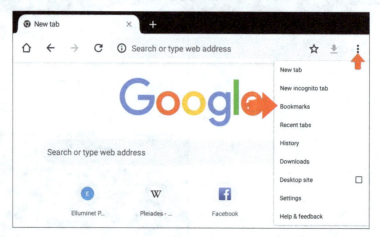

Chrome puts all your bookmarked sites in to the 'mobile bookmarks' folder. Tap on this folder to open it up.

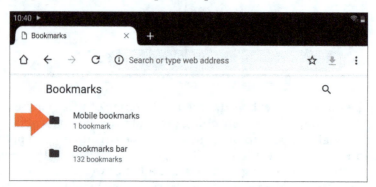

Tap on the name of the site in the list to return to the website.

Add Website to Chrome Start Page

You can add all your most used websites to the start page on Chrome. To do this, first you need to navigate to the page you want to add. Tap the three dots icon on the top right, and select 'add to home screen'.

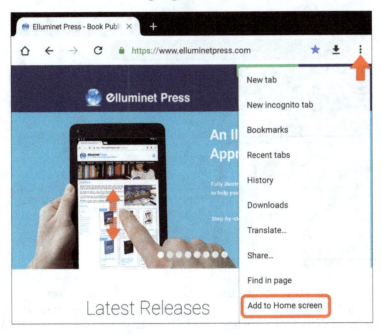

Edit the name if you need to, then tap 'add'.

Tap 'add'. This will also add the icon to your tablet's home screen.

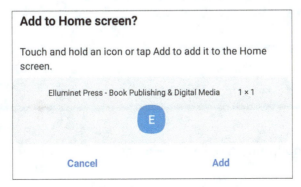

Translate a Page

This feature is useful if you come across a webpage that isn't in English, or you want to translate the page into another language. To do this, tap the three dots icon on the top right, then select 'translate...'

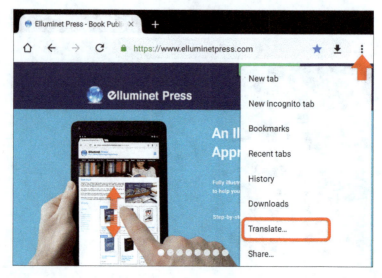

From the panel that opens up on the bottom of the screen, you'll see the current language and the language Chrome is translating the website into. To select another language, tap the three dots icon on the right hand side of the panel.

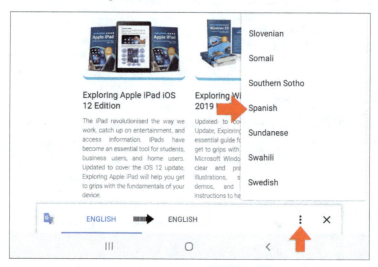

From the popup menu, select the language you want to translate the page into.

Share a Page

You can share the page you're on with a friend or colleague. You can share via email, social media, Hangouts message, or cloud drive. To do this, first navigate to the page you want to share, then tap the three dots icon on the top right. From the drop down menu, tap 'share'.

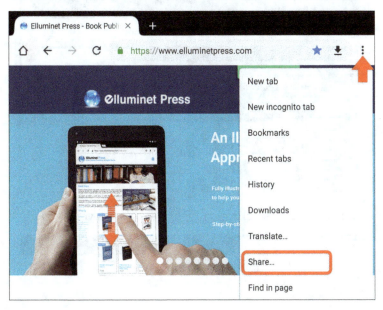

Select the method you want to use to share the page. Eg email, or facebook.

Fill in an email address if you're sharing via email, or post if you're sharing via facebook.

Browsing History

You can see a list of websites you have visited. To see this, click the '3 dots' icon on the top right. From the menu that appears, select 'history'.

Here you'll see a reverse chronological list of sites you've visited.

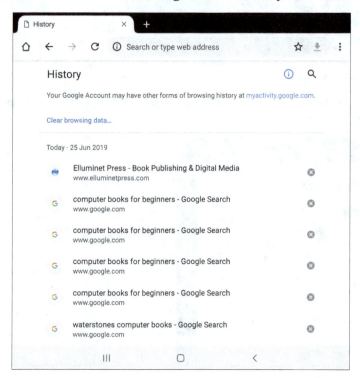

Tap on one in the list to revisit the site. Scroll down to see more in the list.

Downloads

If you have downloaded photos, files, or web pages for offline viewing, you'll find them here in the downloads folder. To get to your downloads, click the '3 dots' icon on the top right. From the menu that appears, select 'downloads'.

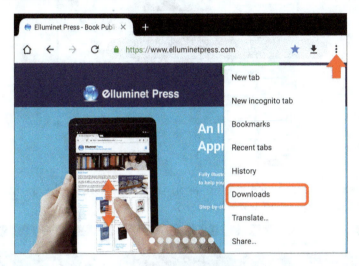

Here you'll see a reverse chronological list of items you've downloaded.

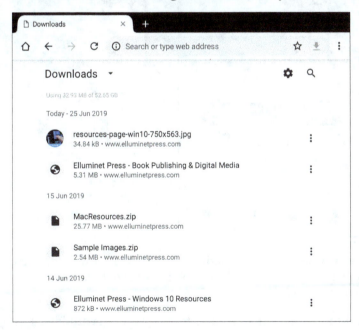

Tap on an item in the list to open it up.

85

Desktop vs Mobile Site

Click the '3 dots' icon on the top right. From the menu that appears, select 'desktop site'. If the box is checked, this will return the desktop version of the site, if not Chrome will return the mobile version.

Here below, we can see the desktop version of our website on the left and the mobile version on the right.

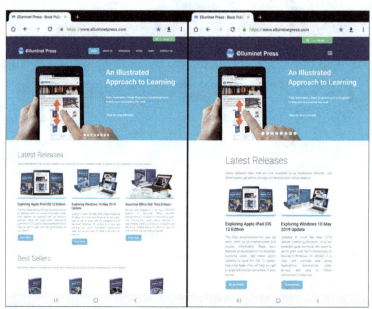

The mobile version is designed to run on devices with smaller screens such as smart phones or small tablets, and makes it easier to navigate using your finger.

The desktop version is designed to run on larger tablets, laptops and desktop computers with point and click navigation rather than a touch screen.

Chrome will auto detect this on smaller tablets and phones, and return the mobile version of the site by default.

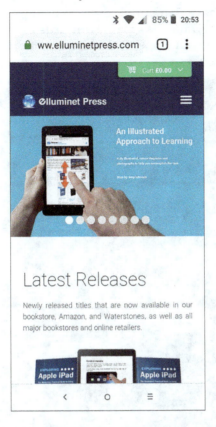

Chrome will auto detect this on larger tablets, laptops or desktops, and return the desktop version of the site by default.

Using Gmail

The Galaxy Tabs have Samsung's own email app, however I find Gmail is better. To open Gmail, swipe downwards from the middle of the screen to reveal all your apps. If Gmail isn't there, you will find it in a folder called 'Google'.

To make Gmail more accessible, tap and hold your finger on the Gmail icon, then select 'add to home'.

This will add the Gmail icon to your home screen, so you can launch the browser without going through the 'all apps' screen.

When Gmail opens you'll land on the main screen.

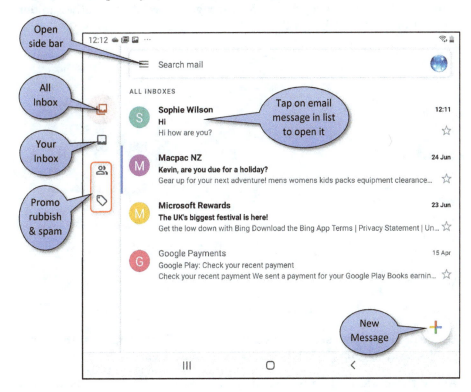

Reading your Email

To open or reply to an email, make sure you've selected the 'all inboxes' icon from the left hand panel, then tap the email you want from the list on the right. Emails in bold are unread.

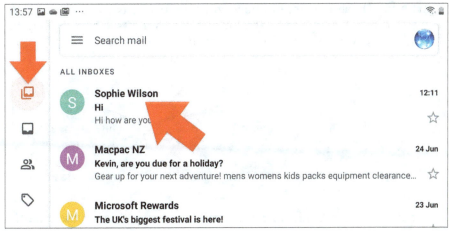

The email will open up. Along the top you'll see some icons. Here you can archive a message, delete a message, move it to another folder, print it out, or even block the user.

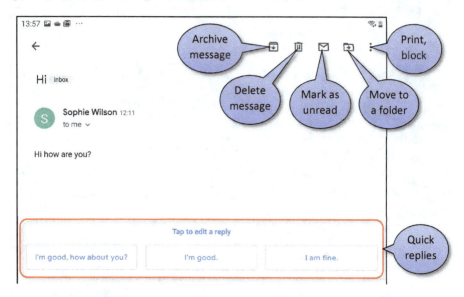

Underneath you'll see a message header. This contains the email subject, date/time and the sender's email address.

Along the bottom of your screen, you'll see some quick replies. These are automatically generated depending on what the email says. You can tap on these if you want to send a reply quickly.

Replying to an Email

Once you've opened an email, along the bottom, you'll see some shortcuts. These shortcuts allow you to reply directly to the sender, reply to all which includes any multiple recipients who received the email, and forward the email message to another user.

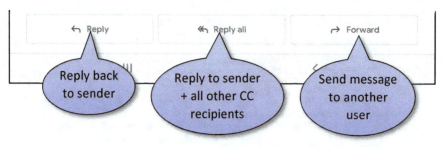

In most cases, tap 'reply' to reply directly to the sender of the email.

Type your reply at the top of the message.

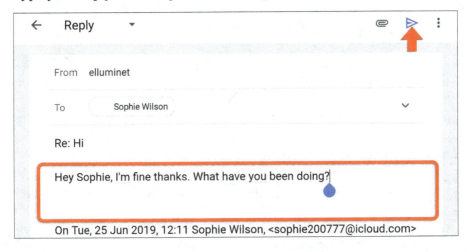

Tap the send icon on the top right when you're done.

Forward an Email

To forward an email, tap on the message in your inbox. Then tap the 'forward email' icon on the top right of the email message.

Enter the email addresses of the people you want to forward the message to.

Start to type them into the 'to' field. If these people are in your contacts, you'll see their names and email addresses pop up. Tap on these to insert the full email address.

Type in a message at the top if you need to.

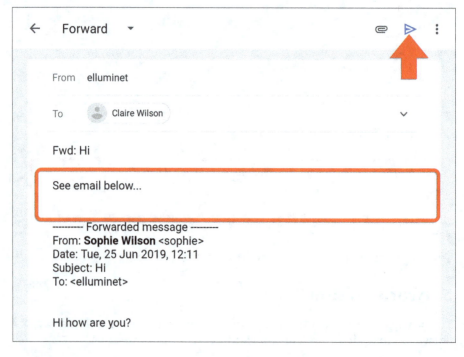

Tap the send icon on the top right when you're done.

New Message

To start a new message, tap the '+' icon on the bottom right of the screen.

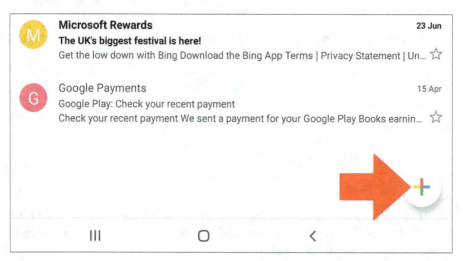

This will bring up a new email. Tap in the 'To:' field to enter an email address.

In the 'to' field, start typing the person's name, then select the email address from the suggestions. If the person you're emailing isn't in your contacts, you'll need to type in the full email address.

Add a subject in the 'subject' field. This is usually what the email message is about.

In the 'compose email' field, start typing your email message.

Tap the 'send' icon on the top right to send your message.

Add an Attachment

You can attach documents, images or photos to your emails. To do this, start a new email or reply to an email message.

Write your email as normal. To add an attachment, tap the attachment icon on the top right of the message.

From the popup menu on the top right, select **'insert from drive'** if the file you want is stored on your Google Drive, such as a document.

Select **'attach file'** if the file you want is stored on your tablet - use this if the file you want is a photo or video you've taken with your tablet's camera.

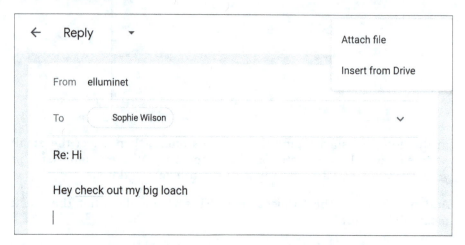

Select the file you want. In this example, I'm attaching a photograph of my loach fish to send to Sophie.

Your attachment(s) will appear at the bottom of your message.

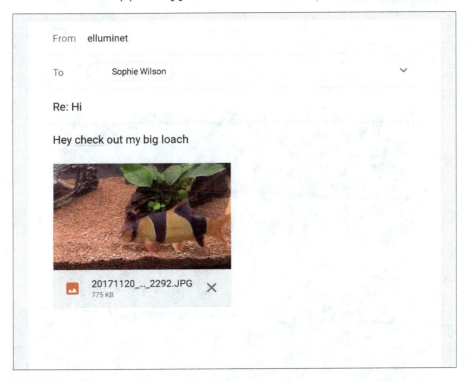

Tap the 'send' icon on the top right to send your message.

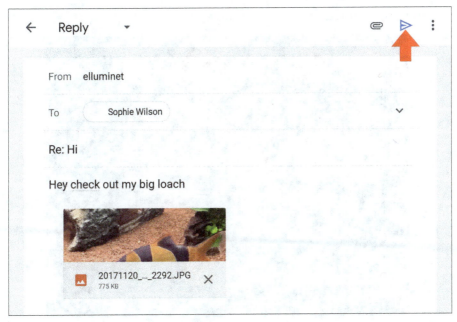

Contacts

The contacts app is your address book and contains your contact's email addresses, phone numbers and addresses. Samsung have produced their own contacts app which works pretty well. To start the app, swipe downwards from the middle of the screen to reveal all your apps.

Tap on the contacts icon to start the app.

View Contact Details

Once the contacts app opens, down the left hand side you'll see a list of all the people you have contact information for. You can scroll up and down the list using your finger. Tap on one of the names to view or edit the details for that person.

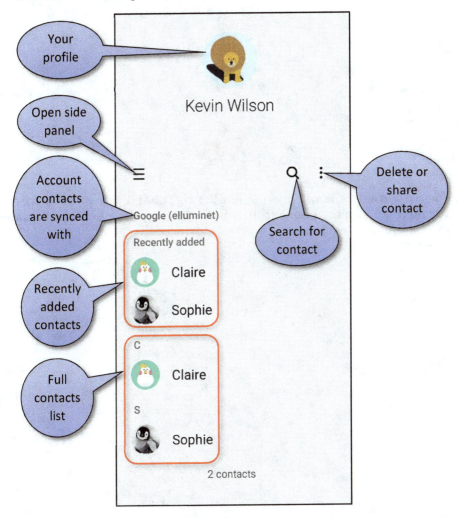

At the very top of the window, you'll see your own profile. Here you can edit your own contact information, as well as share it with other people.

You can also open the side panel. From here you can change the account your contacts are synced with, as well as manage your contacts - merge or import from another source.

To view a person's contact details, tap on their name in the list on the left hand side. I'm going to tap on my contact 'Claire' in my list.

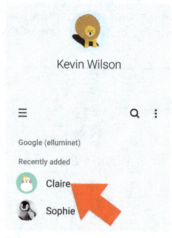

The person's details will open up on the right hand side of the screen. To call them, tap the phone icon, tap the message icon or email icon to send them a message.

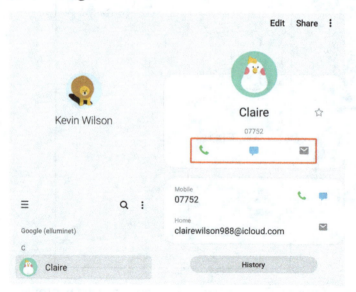

From the icons along the top right, tap 'edit' to edit the person's details, eg if they've changed their number or email address. Tap 'share' to send the contact details to another person. Use the three dots icon to open the drop down options menu. Here you can delete the contact, or link to another contact.

Tap 'history' to see all the correspondence you've had with this person.

Edit Details

Open the calendar app, then tap on the name of the person in the list whose details you want to change.

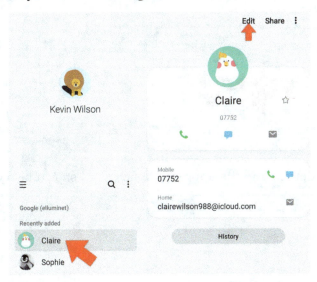

Tap on the field you want to change. In this example I'm adding a work phone number. Enter the changes using the on screen keyboard.

Tap 'save' at the bottom of the screen when you're finished to save the changes.

99

Add New Contact

You can add a new contact from scratch using the contacts app. To do this, open the contacts app then tap the orange '+' icon on the bottom of the screen.

Enter the details into the appropriate fields, as shown below.

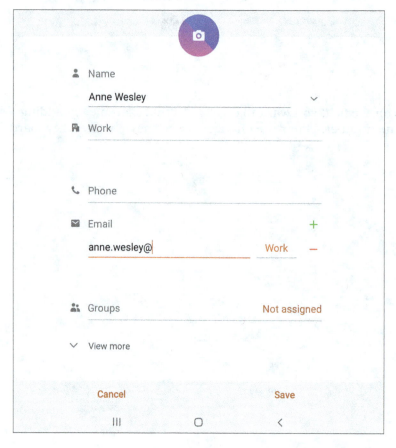

Tap 'save' at the bottom of the screen to save the details..

Add Contact from Message

You can add a new contact from the Hangouts app or the Gmail app

Open the email, then tap on the small icon next to the person's name on the top left hand side.

This will open up the person's contact details. To add these to your contacts, tap the 'add contact' icon on the bottom right of the screen.

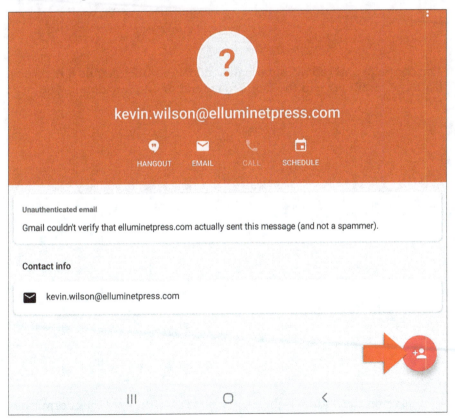

From the prompt, select the account you want to store the contact detail in. Most often this will be your Google account, so select 'Google' then tap 'set as default' (you'll only need to do this once).

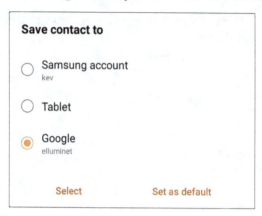

Tap 'create contact'.

The contacts app will automatically add the contact details it extracted from the profile. Tap in the fields to amend or add any details you need to.

Tap 'save' on the bottom right hand side to save the contact information.

Calendar

The calendar app allows you to keep track of events and appointments. You can add reminders, create appointments and events, so you never miss anything.. Samsung have produced their own calendar app which works pretty well. To start the app, swipe downwards from the middle of the screen to reveal all your apps.

Tap on the calendar icon to start the app.

When the calendar app opens, you'll see your calendar with any events or appointments that have been added.

Calendar View

You can change the calendar view to show appointments and events by month, week or day - as shown below.

You can view your appointments by year or month...

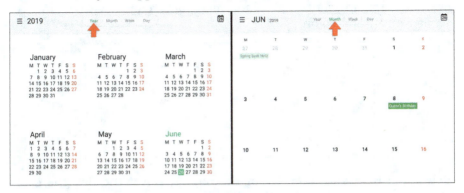

...as well as by week or day. Just select the option from the panel along the top of the screen.

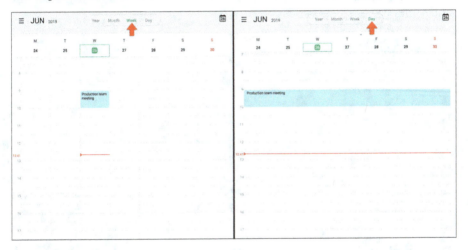

Add Event

To add a new event, reminder or appointment, on the main screen tap the 'green plus icon' on the bottom right of your screen.

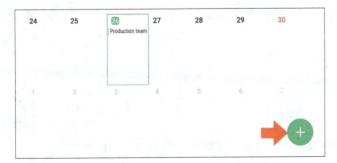

In the field at the top of the screen, start typing in the name of the event or appointment. Eg "team meeting", "coffee with claire", or "conference", and so on.

Select the time and date. From the popup, select the day the event starts on from the calendar, then below select the time from the rollers. Then do the same for the end time. Tap 'end' on the top right, select a date the appointment ends, then use the rollers below to select the end time.

Tap 'done' on the bottom right of the screen.

Tap where it says '10 minutes before' then select how far in advance you want to be reminded from the options.

Tap 'save' on the bottom right when you're finished.

Google Hangouts

Google Hangouts is Google's answer to video chat. You can chat one to one with someone or have a group chat. You can call anyone on a tablet, ChromeBook, laptop, phone or pc that has Google Hangouts and a webcam on the device. You can also send instant messages, photographs, and videos.

To start the Google Hangouts, swipe downwards from the middle of the screen to reveal all your apps.

Tap the 'Google' folder, then tap 'Hangouts'.

When Hangouts opens up, you'll see a list of contacts you've been in contact with. If you use Hangouts a lot, you'll find all your most recent contacts listed here.

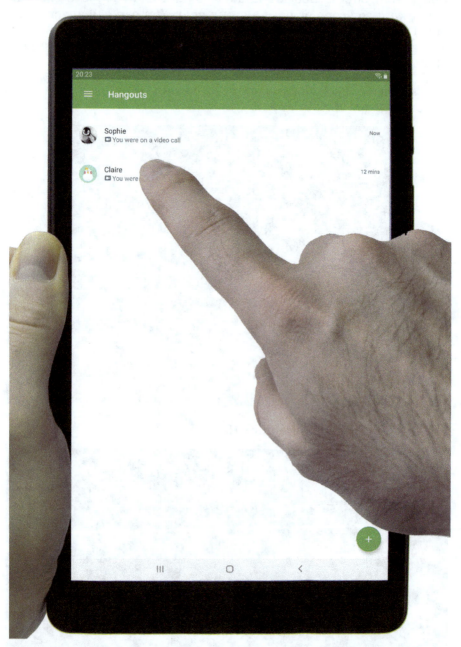

Tap on the names to see the conversations you've had with these contacts.

Calling New Contacts

To contact someone new, click the green '+' icon on the bottom right.

From the popup menu select 'new video call' if you want to use the video chat option. In this example, I'm going to place a video call. So select 'new video call'.

Select the person's name from your contact list. If the name isn't there, type their Gmail address, name or number into the search field at the top.

Remember the other person will need to have a Google / Gmail Account and the Hangouts App installed on their device. Inviting users without Google / Gmail accounts at the time of writing no longer works for the free version of Hangouts.

If the person has the Hangouts app, they'll get a prompt on their device telling them who's calling. If you're using your tablet and it is unlocked, you'll see the prompt appear on the top of your screen. Tap 'answer' to answer the call.

If your tablet is locked, you'll see the call prompt on the lock screen.

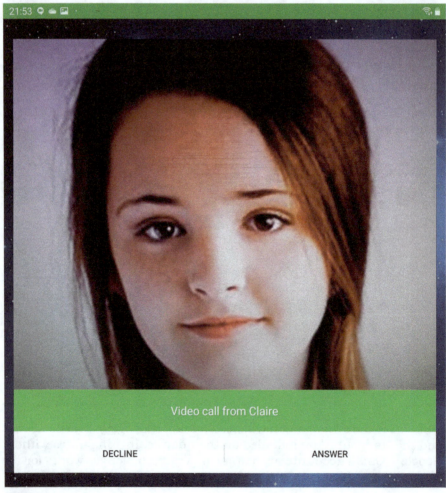

Video Calls

If you've had a conversation with someone before, you'll see their name listed in the recent contacts list when you open Hangouts. Tap on one of these names to see the conversations you've had. In this demo, Sophie is going to place a call to Claire from her Galaxy tablet. To place the call, tap on the name in the list.

This will open up your conversation window with that person. To place a video call, tap the small camera icon on the top right.

When you place the call, you'll see an image of your webcam in the main viewer, while you are waiting for the other person to answer.

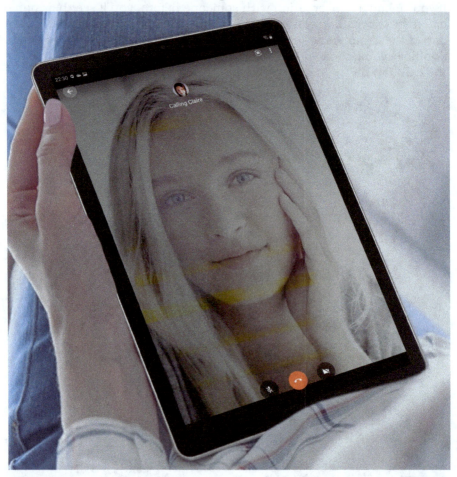

Make sure you appear fully in the frame as shown above.

The other person will get a prompt allowing them to either accept or decline the call.

When the other person answers, you'll see a live image of them in your main viewer. You'll also see a preview of your own camera on the bottom right of your screen, as you can see on Sophie's tablet below.

Along the bottom of your screen, you'll also see three buttons. These usually disappear during a call - just tap the screen to bring them up.

The button on the far left mutes your microphone so the person you're talking to can't hear you. Similarly the icon on the far right turns off your camera. Useful if you want a moment's privacy.

The red button in the middle closes your video call.

Similarly, Claire will see Sophie in her main viewer. She could also be anywhere in the world that has an internet connection.

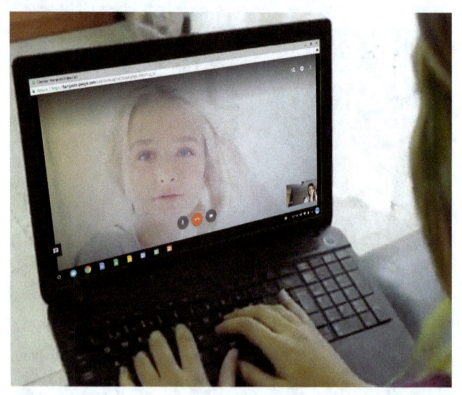

This is useful for keeping in touch with friends and family all over the world.

These calls are also free to make and you can chat as long as you like - you'll still have to pay for your internet connection though, whether that is through cable, broadband, wifi or cellular depending on your service provider.

Sending Messages

With Hangouts you can also send instant messages. To send a new message, tap the '+' icon on the bottom right, then select 'new conversation' from the popup.

Select the person you want to send a message to, or type their email address into the field at the top of the screen. Note, using the free version of Hangouts, the person you're sending a message to will need to have a Gmail or Google Account.

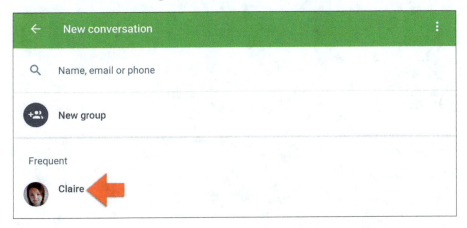

In the window that appears, you'll be able to type your message using the on screen keyboard at the bottom of the screen or an external keyboard.

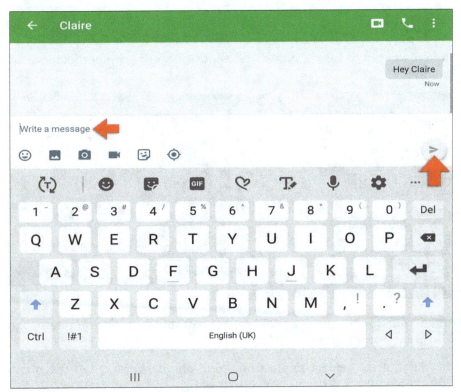

You can also send emojis, photos, videos, and stickers. To do this, select the options from the icon bar under the message field.

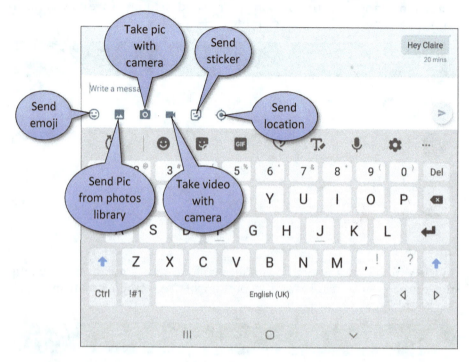

If you wanted to take a photo and send it, tap the camera icon on the icon bar

Take your photo, then tap 'ok' at the bottom. To send the photo, tap the green send button.

If you want to send a photo from your photos library, tap the photo library icon from the icon panel instead.

116

Messages

If you have the LTE version of the Galaxy Tab, ie the one where you can insert a SIM card, you can send text messages using the messages app. Note if you have the WiFi only version of the Galaxy Tab, you'll only be able to send messages to those who have Gmail email accounts.

To start the app, swipe downwards from the middle of the screen to reveal all your apps.

Tap on the messages icon to start the app.

Sending Messages

Tap the 'new message' icon.

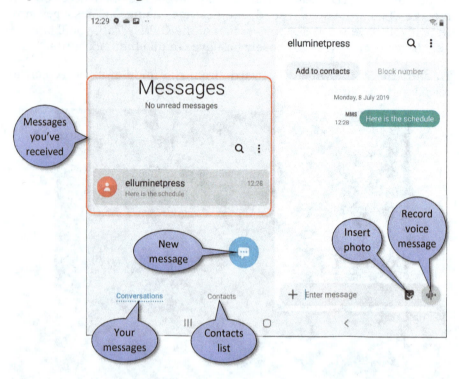

Add the recipient's name in the field at the top. Tap the icon to the right of the field to select the recipient's name from your contacts list. Then enter your message.

Send a Voice Message

To record and send a voice message, tap and hold Record , say your message, and then release your finger.

Tap send icon to send the message.

Send a Picture or Video

Tap the '+' icon on the left hand side of the message box.

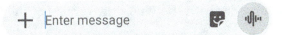

Select the image you want to send from your gallery, or tap the camera icon to take a picture/video with your camera.

Tap the send icon when ready to send.

Phone

If you have the LTE version of the Galaxy Tab, ie the one where you can insert a SIM card, you can make phone calls using the phone app. Note that this doesn't work with the WiFi only version of the Galaxy Tab.

To start the app, swipe downwards from the middle of the screen to reveal all your apps.

Tap on the messages icon to start the app.

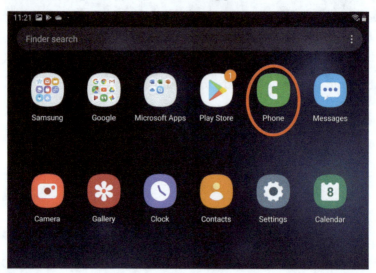

Here you can enter a phone number using the keypad.

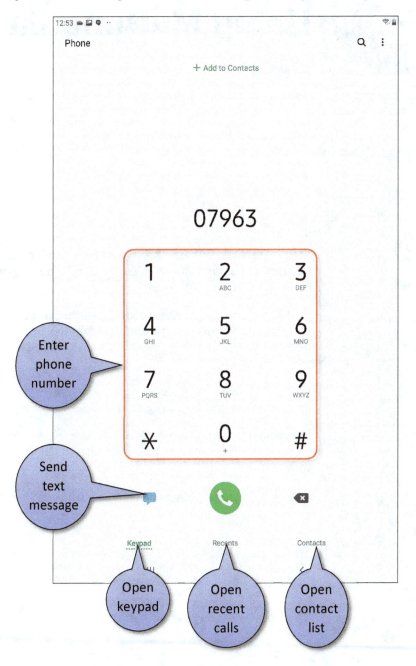

Or you can open your recent calls and call the person back just by tapping on their message. You can also place a new call using your contacts list.

Using Multimedia

Your Galaxy Tablet has a large collection of multimedia apps available. These can be downloaded from the Google Play Store.

In this section we'll take a look at taking photos with your camera app - try panoramic photos or portrait photos. We'll also take a look at enhancing photos you've taken.

We'll also have a look at downloading movies, tv programmes and listening to music.

For this section, have a look at the video demos. Open your web browser and navigate to the following website:

www.elluminetpress.com/galaxyamm

Camera App

You'll find the camera app on your home screen. Swipe downwards from the middle of the screen to reveal all your apps

Tap on the camera icon to start the app.

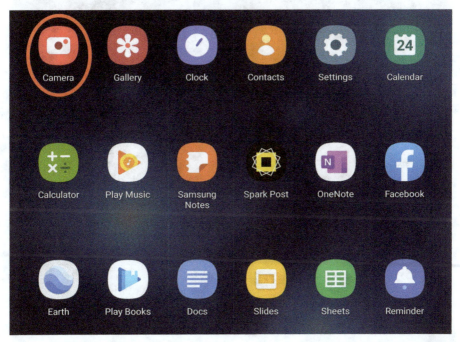

Chapter 5: Using Multimedia

When the camera app opens up, you'll see a live preview of the camera on your screen. This is equivalent to the view finder or LCD screen on a digital camera - use this to line up your shot.

Taking Pictures

Taking pictures is simply a matter of lining up your scene or subject on the screen of your tablet. You can hold your tablet vertically as shown in the illustration below, or you can hold it horizontally depending on what you're trying to shoot.

Tap on the screen to focus on a specific point if you need to.

Once you've lined up your shot, tap the shutter button to take the photo, as shown above.

Once you take a photo, you'll see a preview thumbnail icon of the last image taken, on the right hand side under the shutter button. Tap on this thumbnail to view the photo in the photos app.

Panoramic Photos

Panoramic photos are great for landscapes and scenery.

To take a panoramic shot, select 'panorama' from the list along the bottom of the screen.

Now position your camera at the start of the scene - eg, the beginning of this mountain range on the left - then tap the shutter icon.

Now move your camera along the mountain range until you get to the end. You'll see the panoramic indicator in the centre of the screen fill up as you do so. This indicates how much of the image the camera has captured. Keep going until you reach the end of the scene.

Make sure you stand in one spot, the panoramic photos don't work if you walk along with your tablet.

Tap the stop button on the right hand side to finish.

Chapter 5: Using Multimedia

Zoom

To zoom, use your forefinger and thumb to pinch the screen. This will zoom out.

To zoom in, use your forefinger and thumb. Move your forefinger and thumb apart.

Do this to zoom in and out on a specific part of the photograph.

Focus

Your tablet will automatically try to focus on the subject, but you can force the camera to focus on another point if you need to. To set the focus point, use your forefinger to tap on the part of the photograph you want to focus on.

Tap and hold your finger to lock focus until you see the yellow circle.

Exposure

Your tablet will attempt to automatically select the correct exposure for your photo. However, if for some reason your photo is too bright or too dark, you can adjust the exposure manually. To do this, tap and hold your finger on the screen until you see the yellow focus lock icon.

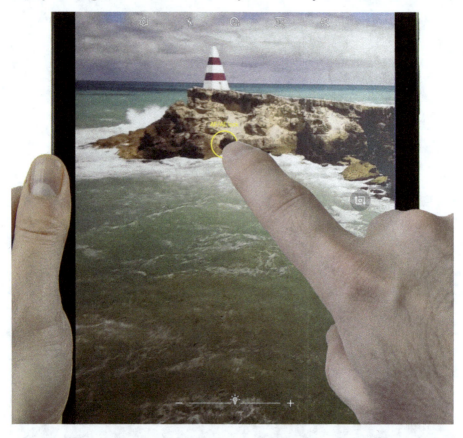

Along the bottom of the screen, you'll see a slider. Drag this slider to the left to darken the image, drag it to the right to brighten the image up.

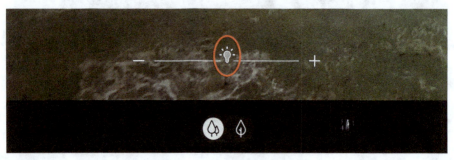

Stickers & Stamps

Stickers are small graphics and animations you can superimpose over your photographs or videos. These graphics could be glasses, hats, ears, food, and so on. The graphics will also track your movements, so as you move your face, the sticker will respond and move with you. To add a sticker to your photo, select 'photo' from the options along the bottom of the screen.

Tap 'sticker' on the top right.

Switch to your front facing camera using the icon on the right, then select a sticker from the panel that opens up along the bottom of the screen.

131

Chapter 5: Using Multimedia

You can also add fancy text and other graphics. To do this, select the stamps icon from the three small icons on the bottom left of your screen. Then select a stamp.

Tap on the screen to apply the stamp. You can tap and drag the stamp to any position on the screen.

When you tap on the stamp, you'll see a white box appear with four dots around the corners. These are resize handles. Tap and drag the handles to resize the stamp.

To delete a stamp, tap the dot on the top right of the white box.

Recording Video

To start recording video, select 'video' from the options along the bottom of the screen.

Most of the time videos look the best when recorded with your tablet in landscape orientation, as shown above. Tap the record button to start recording.

You'll see a counter appear at the bottom - this records the duration of the video.

You can also zoom in and out. To zoom out, pinch the screen with your thumb and forefinger. To zoom in, do the reverse: spread your thumb and forefinger.

To set the focus point, tap on the screen (on the object you want to focus on)...

To stop recording, tap the record button (or stop button) again.

Samsung Gallery App

With the Samsung Gallery App you can manage, store and enhance the photographs you take with your camera. You'll find the app icon on your home screen. Swipe downwards from the middle of the screen to reveal all your apps

Tap on the gallery icon to start the app.

Chapter 5: Using Multimedia

Along the bottom of the main screen you'll see four icons. Use these to access the different sections of the photos app. Tap 'pictures' to see all the photos on your tablet.

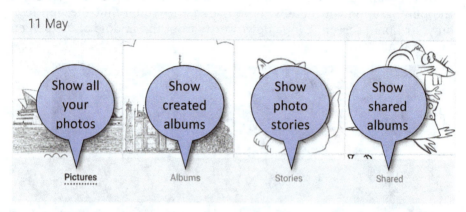

Tap on a photo to open it up.

Here, you'll see a full preview of the photo. Tap the edit icon from the four icons along the bottom of the screen.

Along the bottom of the edit screen you'll see six icons.

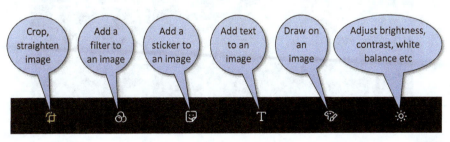

Crop, straighten image

Add a filter to an image

Add a sticker to an image

Add text to an image

Draw on an image

Adjust brightness, contrast, white balance etc

Crop & Straighten

From the edit screen, tap the crop icon from the panel along the bottom of the edit screen.

Around the image you'll see four crop handles, tap and drag these around the part of the image you want to keep.

Tap 'save' on the top right to save the image.

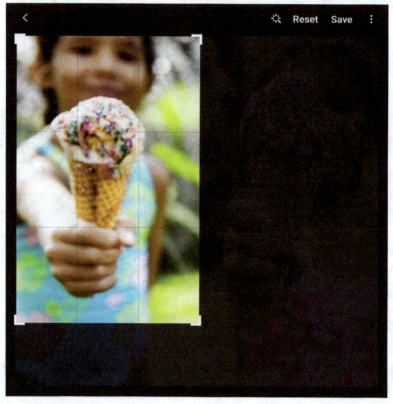

You'll also see five icons along the top half of the panel on the bottom of the screen. Here, you can rotate the image, mirror the image, set a crop aspect ratio, correct the horizontal or vertical perspective, as well isolate a part of the image.

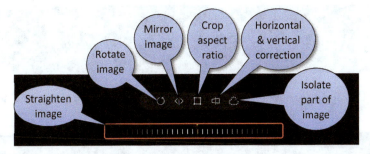

Use the slider along the bottom of the panel to straighten up the image.

Horizontal & Vertical Correction

Tap the crop icon from the panel along the bottom of the edit screen, then tap the 'horizontal & vertical correction' icon from the row of five icons along the top of the panel on the bottom of the screen. Now take a look at the cathedral photo on the left, the walls are distorted.

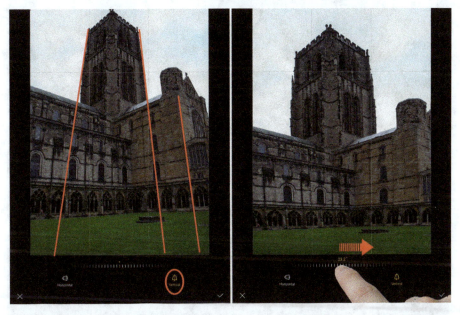

To correct this, tap 'vertical' on the bottom right (because we want to correct the vertical edges of the building). Tap and drag the slider to the right until the walls are straight. Tap the tick on the bottom right to save the changes.

Add a Filter

From the edit screen, tap the filter icon from the panel along the bottom of the edit screen.

From the filter presets panel along the bottom of the screen, select a filter.

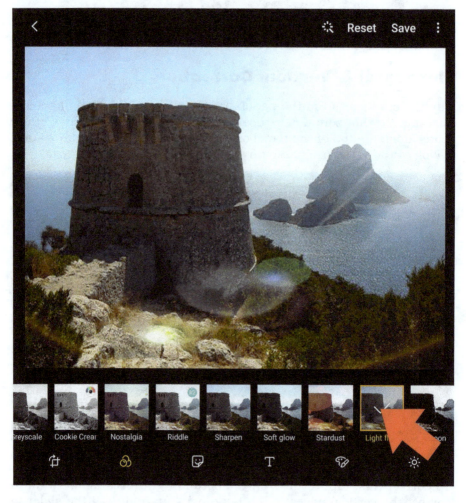

Tap 'save' on the top right to save the changes. Tap 'reset' to reset the image back to its original state.

140

Stickers

From the edit screen, tap the filter icon from the panel along the bottom of the edit screen.

From the panel that opens up along the bottom of the screen, select a sticker. Stickers and stamps are organised into categories, you can select a category from the icons along the bottom.

Select a sticker or stamp from the options.

You can resize the sticker using the resize handles on each corner of the white box. Tap and drag the sticker to move it into position.

Tap the '-' icon on the top right of the white box to delete the sticker.

Tap 'save' on the top right to save the changes.

Adding Text

From the edit screen, tap the filter icon from the panel along the bottom of the edit screen.

Type in your message using the onscreen keyboard.

Tap on the image to accept the text. Now, you can tap and drag the text box into position. Tap 'save' on the top right to save the changes.

Annotate Images

From the edit screen, tap the filter icon from the panel along the bottom of the edit screen.

Tap the pen icon to select a pen. Select a pen and a colour, then a thickness.

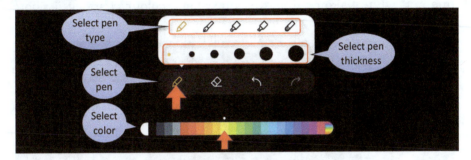

Write your message on the photo with your finger.

Tap 'save' on the top right to save the changes.

Adjusting Images

From the edit screen, tap the filter icon from the panel along the bottom of the edit screen.

Use the options on the panel along the bottom of the screen to adjust brightness, exposure, contrast, saturation (intensity of the colours), hue and white balance (removes unrealistic colour casts eg if photo looks a bit blue or orange).

For each option, a slider will appear underneath the image. Drag this slider left or right to adjust the image.

Tap 'save' on the top right to save the changes.

Google Photos App

With the photos app you can manage, store and enhance the photographs you take with your camera. You can also share photos on social media, or send them to friends and family.

To start the photos app, swipe downwards from the middle of the screen to reveal all your apps

Tap the 'Google' folder, then tap 'Photos'.

Chapter 5: Using Multimedia

Along the bottom of the main screen you'll see four icons. Use these to access the different sections of the photos app.

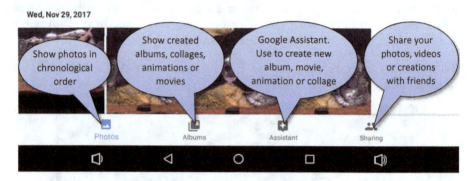

If you select the 'photos' section, you'll see a list of thumbnails ordered by date.

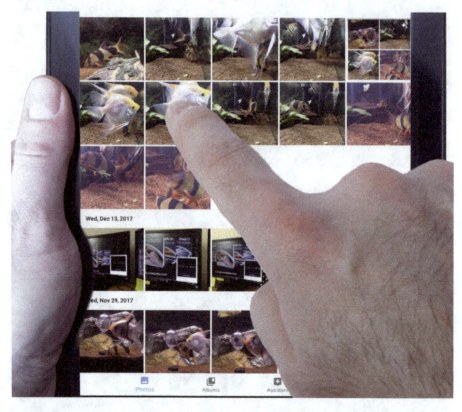

Any photos you've taken will appear in this section, as shown above. Scroll up and down with your finger to scan through all your photos.

You can tap on any of the thumbnails to view or edit the photo.

Once you've opened a photo, you'll see it appear in the main section of the screen.

From here, you'll see some icons along the bottom. The one on the far left allows you to share the photo on social media, hangouts, email or google drive.

The next one along allows you to add filters as well as crop and enhance your images.

Google lens search analyses the image and does a google search on the web for images and articles relating to the content of the image.

The one on the end deletes the image.

Adjusting Images

You can adjust brightness and contrast of your images. This is useful if a photo you have taken has come out dark.

To adjust an image, select one from the 'photos' section on the main screen to open it up.

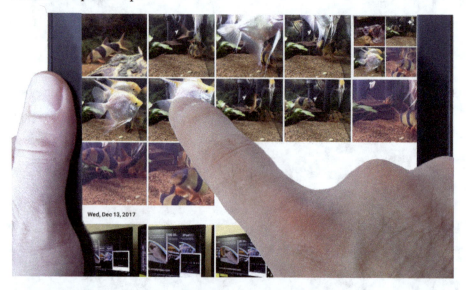

Tap the adjust icon on the bottom left to reveal the adjustment options.

You'll see a panel open along the bottom. Select the second icon from the left - the brightness and contrast controls.

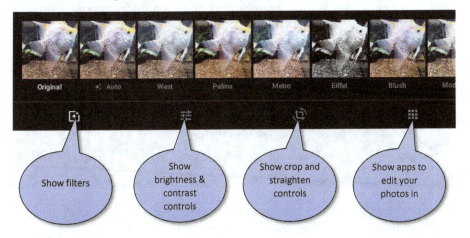

You'll see three sliders appear along the bottom. Click the small arrows on the right hand side to expand the 'light' and 'color' controls.

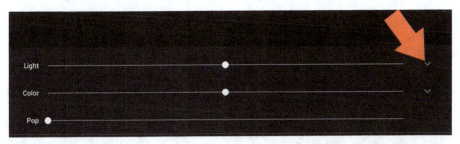

The 'light' controls adjust exposure, shadows and highlights independently. Use 'exposure' to adjust the overall brightness of the photo. Use 'whites' and 'highlights' to adjust only the bright parts. Use 'blacks' and 'shadows' to adjust only the dark parts of the image.

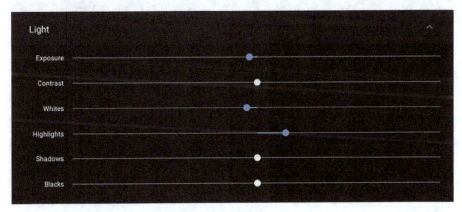

Chapter 5: Using Multimedia

Now open up the 'color' controls. Experiment with the controls until you get the desired look on your photos. Make the colours bolder using the 'saturation' slider, or enhance skin tones on portrait photos of group photos using the 'skin tone' slider.

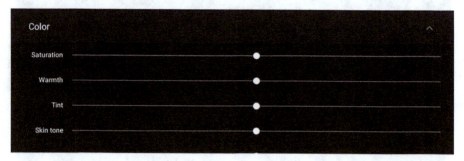

If your image has a blue or orange tint, try the 'warmth', 'tint' or 'deep blue' sliders.

Crop an Image

To crop an image, select one from the 'photos' section on the main screen to open it up. From the icons along the bottom, select the second icon from the left.

From the icons on the bottom of the screen, select the second one from the right.

When in crop mode, you'll see four crop marks in each of the four corners of the image. Tap and drag these corners inwards, so the crop mask highlights the area of the image you want to keep.

Tap 'done' on the bottom right of your screen to confirm the crop. Then tap 'save' on the top right of your screen to save the changes to your image.

Creating Collages

You can select a maximum of 9 images for a collage. To create a collage, tap the 'assistant' icon on the bottom right.

Select 'collage' from the options along the top.

You can select from the 'photos' section on the next screen. To select the images, tap the small circle on the top left of the image thumbnail.

Once you've done that, tap 'create' on the top right.

The photos app will generate a collage with the photographs you have selected. Tap the 'back arrow' at the bottom to go back to the main screen.

You'll fine all the collages you have created in the 'album' section.

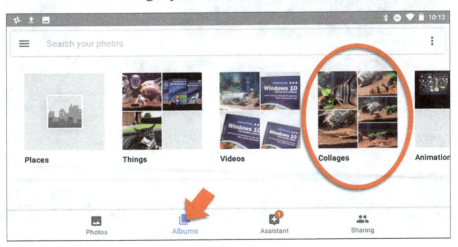

Sharing Photos

You can share any of your videos, photos, and collages with friends and family via hangouts, messaging, or email.

First, select the photos you want to share from the 'photos' section of the photos app.

Tap and hold your finger on one of the images you want. You'll see some 'selection circles' appear on the top left of each of the image thumbnails. Tap on these 'selection circles' to select more images.

Once you have done that, tap the 'share' icon on the top right of the screen.

Sharing Image as a Link

From your contact options, select the person you want to share the images with. You can either type the email address or phone number into the search field at the top, or select from your most recent contacts.

If the contact isn't listed on this screen, tap 'more' to view all your contacts.

This will send the person a link to the images you have shared with them. They'll receive this as an email or a text message, depending on what contact details you have entered for that particular person. In this example, the message was sent to the person as an email.

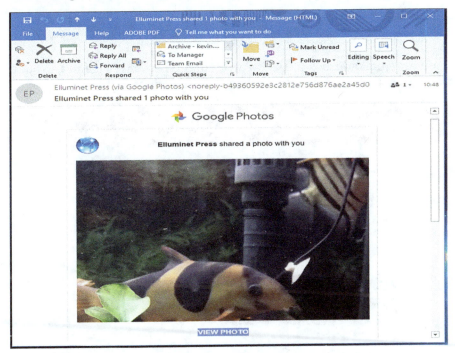

Note that the images themselves weren't actually sent. Google Photos sends a link for the recipient to view the photos you share. They will need to click on the 'view photos' link in the email to view all the images.

Sharing the Actual Image

You can also share the actual image rather than just a link using one of the other apps available such as hangouts or GMail, as well as directly to someone else's tablet using bluetooth.

In this example, I'm going to send the image as an email attachment. So, select 'GMail' from the bottom of the 'sharing window'.

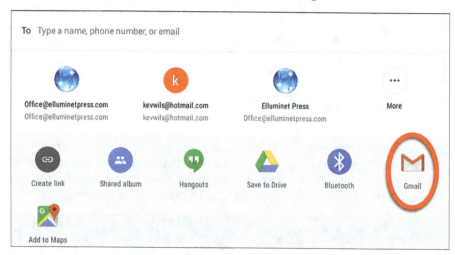

Add an email address in the 'to' field, and type a message in the body. You'll see the image is attached as an attachment.

Tap the 'send' icon on the top right when you're finished.

Play Music

Using the play music app you can purchase individual tracks and albums from the play store, or you can stream any music you like if you subscribe to 'play music'.

To start the app, swipe downwards from the middle of the screen to reveal all your apps

Tap the 'play music' icon.

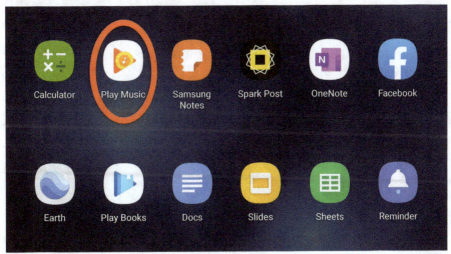

Chapter 5: Using Multimedia

Streaming Music

When you first start the play music app, it will ask you to subscribe to 'play music'. This allows you to listen to any track or album currently available in the music store.

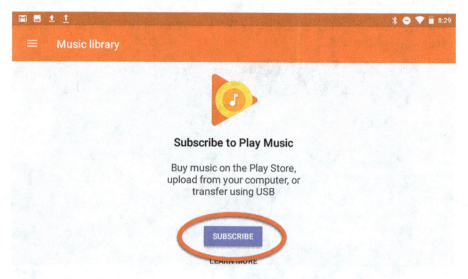

Select an 'individual' plan if you want to stream music to your device. If you want to stream to more than one device select 'family'.

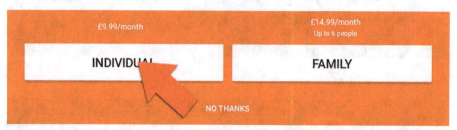

Hit 'continue', then add your payment method and confirm your subscription.

Once you have subscribed, you can browse through all the genres and the latest releases.

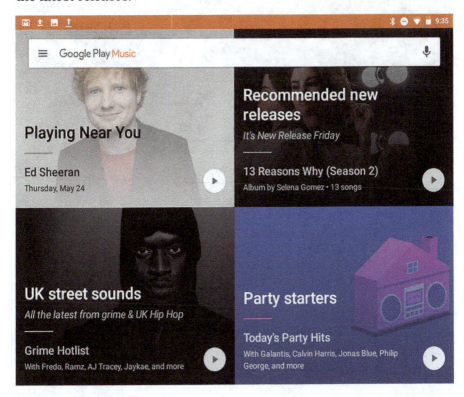

Or you can search for specific artists, albums or tracks.

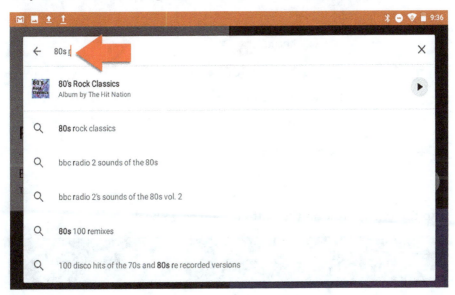

Just tap on the track you want to listen to...

Tap the back arrow on the bottom right to go back.

Creating Playlists

To add a song to a playlist, tap the 3 dots icon next to the track in the list.

From the popup menu select 'add to playlist'.

Select the playlist you want to add the track to from the list. Or tap 'new playlist' to create a new one.

You'll find your playlists in your music library. To open your music library, swipe inwards from the left hand side of your screen to open the sidebar. From the sidebar tap 'music library'.

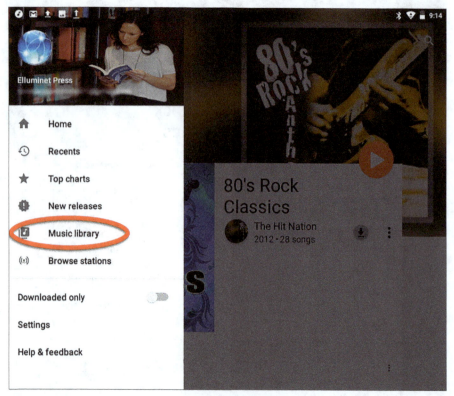

Buying Tracks

If you don't take out the subscription to play music, you can still download individual tracks and albums.

Select the hamburger icon on the top left hand side of the screen. You can also swipe inwards from the left hand edge of your screen.

From the slideout menu, select 'shop' to open the google play store.

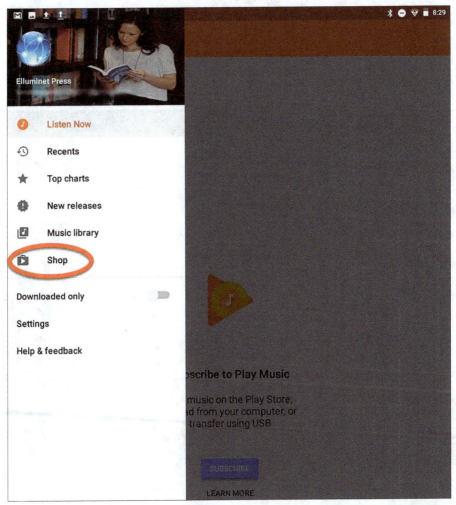

Chapter 5: Using Multimedia

You can search for a track or artist using the search bar at the top of the screen, or you can browse through the categories and latest releases further down the page.

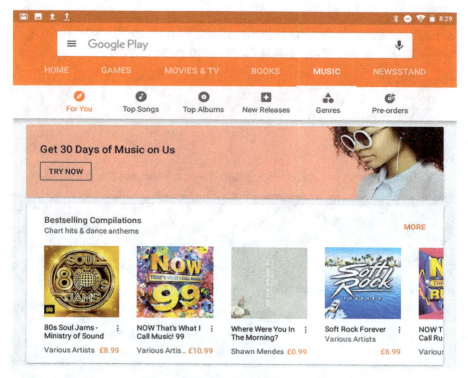

Tap on the front cover of an album or song to view the details.

Tap the price tag to buy the track.

Play Movies & TV

You'll find the play movies & TV app in your app drawer on your home screen.

To start the app, swipe downwards from the middle of the screen to reveal all your apps

Tap the 'Google' folder, then tap 'Play Movies & TV'.

Chapter 5: Using Multimedia

When the app opens, you'll see the main screen. You'll see lists of new releases and top selling movies & TV programmes.

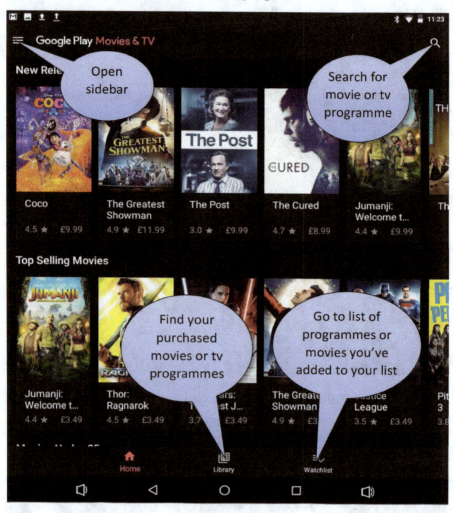

You can tap on any of the covers to view details on each movie or tv programme.

You can also search for a specific title using the search icon on the top right of the screen. Type your search into the field.

In the search results, tap on the show or movie you want. Just tap the cover.

Chapter 5: Using Multimedia

On the screen that appears, you'll see a summary of the movie or series. If you selected a tv series, you'll see a list of episodes. You can either buy individual episodes, or buy the whole series. Just tap on the price tags.

You'll find movies or tv programmes that you have purchased in your video library.

From the main screen select 'library'.

The library is split into two categories: movies & tv shows. In this example I downloaded an episode from a tv show, so I'll select 'tv shows' from the options along the top of the screen.

Now just tap the show you want to watch.

Select the play icon on the thumbnail in the list of episodes.

Using Apps

You can download millions of app from the Play Store. There is an app for almost anything from games to productivity to communication.

Some of these apps are free and some you'll need to pay for.

In this section we'll take a look at using the Play Store to find apps and download them.

For this section, have a look at the video demos. Open your web browser and navigate to the following website:

`www.elluminetpress.com/usingagalaxy`

Play Store

The Play Store has millions of apps available for download direct to your tablet. On the Play Store, you will find everything from games and entertainment to productivity tools such as word processing, drawing and photo apps.

To start the play store app, swipe downwards from the middle of the screen to reveal all your apps

Tap the 'Play Store' icon.

Chapter 6: Using Apps

Once on the Play Store's main screen, at the top you'll see a search bar, here you can search for the app you want if you know the name, eg 'Google docs', 'facebook', 'instagram'; or if you know what type of app you want, eg, 'photo editor', 'word processor', and so on.

Under the search bar, you'll see sections with different types of media for sale.

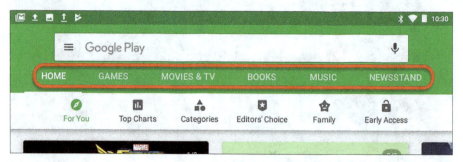

For each section you'll see subsections. Apps and media are further divided into recommendations according to your browsing habits in "for you", then you have top selling apps, editor's choice of apps, categories of apps and so on. These are to help you quickly find the type of media you're looking for.

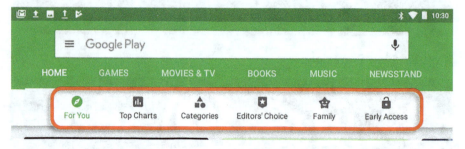

To see all the categories of apps, tap 'categories' and you'll see numerous categories from art and design to lifestyle, productivity and education.

Family apps are apps and games suitable for children, you'll find these in the 'family' section.

The 'early access' section contains apps and games that have just been released or ones that are still in development.

Browse through the sections and explore what is available.

Search for Apps

To find an app, tap on 'Google play' search bar at the bottom of your screen.

Type into the search field on the main screen, as shown below. In this example, I'm going to search for one of my favourite games called 'worms'.

From the suggestions, tap on the closest match.

From the search results, tap on the image to view more details about the app.

Here you'll see reviews, price, screen shots and other info.

To download the app, tap 'install' next to the app if it's free, or tap the price tag if it's paid.

Grant access to the resources the app is requesting, then authorise your payment if prompted.

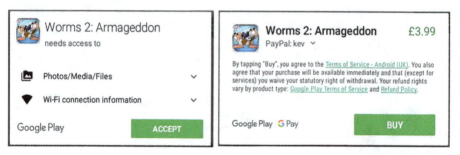

The app will appear on your home screen once it has downloaded and installed itself.

Browsing the Store

If you are more the browsing type, the apps are grouped into categories according to their use. From the Play Store home screen, tap 'categories' from the bar along the top of the screen.

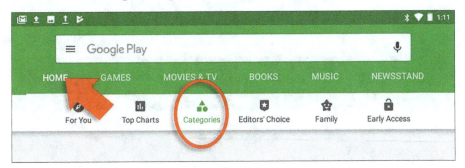

Tap on a category to browse the available apps. In this example, I'm going to explore the 'reference' category.

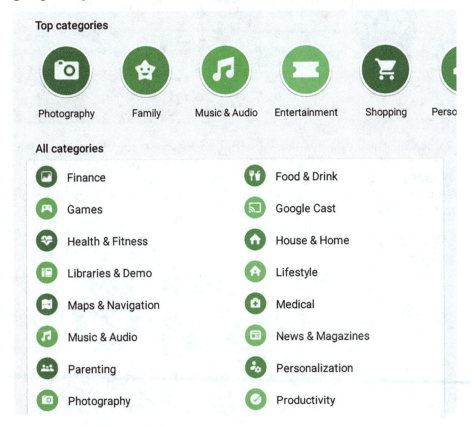

Tap on a category of interest. I'm going to select 'productivity'.

Chapter 6: Using Apps

Here, you'll see a list of all the apps available for that category. You'll see a lot of sections with 'recommended apps', 'apps you might like', 'based on your recent activity' or 'editors choices'. This is Google's attempt at providing you with tailored recommendations of apps you might be interested in.

Swipe across the sections to scroll along these to see if there are any you like.

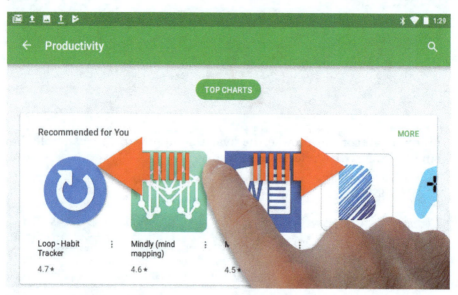

To see all the apps available in that category, scroll down until you see the section name that matches the category you selected. In this example I selected the productivity apps section. When you find this section, tap 'more' on the right hand side to see all the apps available in that category.

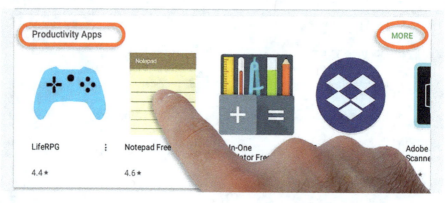

Once you've found an app you want, tap on the image.

This gives you information about what the app does, what it costs, some screen shots of the app in action and the device requirements in order to run the app.

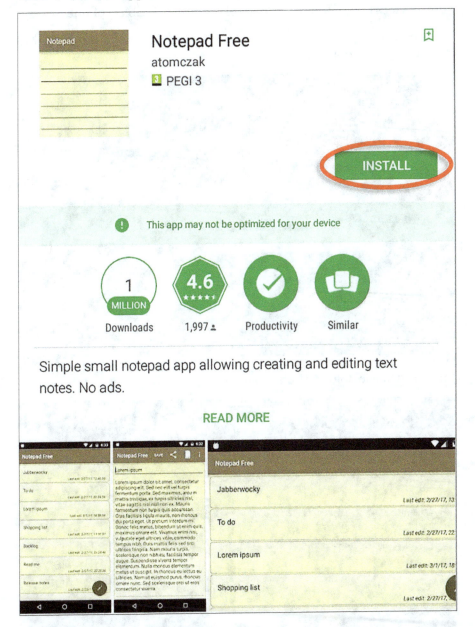

To purchase an app, just tap the price tag if it's a paid app, or tap 'install' if it's free.

You'll find the app installed on your tablet's home screen

Google Drive

Google Drive allows you to store files and synchronize them across all your devices - a laptop, ChromeBook or android tablet/phone.

To start the app, swipe downwards from the middle of the screen to reveal all your apps

Tap the 'Google' folder, then tap 'Drive'.

Once Google Drive opens, you'll see all your files and folders you've saved onto Google Drive. If you don't, select 'files' from the row of icons along the bottom of the screen.

You can tap on any of the thumbnail icons to open the documents.

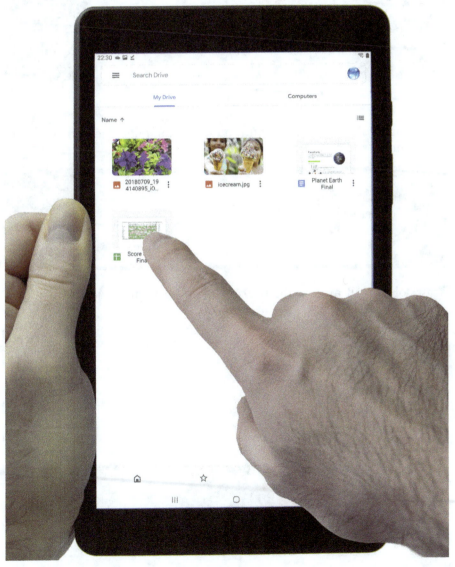

Creating Folders

Creating folders helps you to organise your files into logical groups. To create a folder, tap the '+' icon on the bottom right hand side of your screen. From the popup menu, select 'folder'.

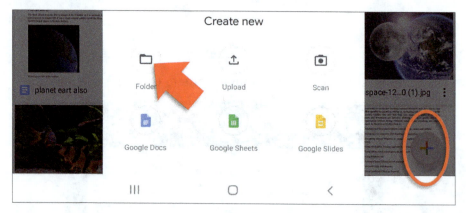

Give your folder a meaningful name. This folder is for my work documents, so I'm going to call it 'work'.

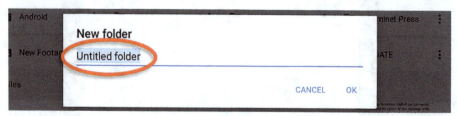

Your folder will appear on the top panel of your Google Drive 'files' screen.

Moving Files

To select multiple files, tap and hold your finger on one of the thumbnails of the files you want to move. You'll see 'tick' icons appear on the bottom left of each thumbnail.

Now tap on each of the files you want - the tick will turn blue to indicate the file has been selected.

Select the 'move' icon from the top right of the screen.

Select the folder you want to move the files into.

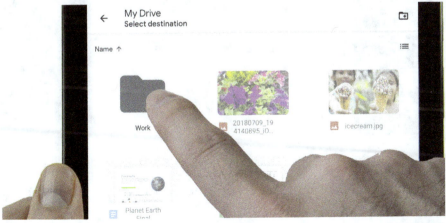

New Documents

To create new documents, tap the '+' icon on the bottom right of the screen.

From the popup menu, along the top, you can create a new folder, upload a file - useful if you're on a laptop or computer and need to upload something to your Google Drive. You can also "scan" hard copy documents into Google Drive.

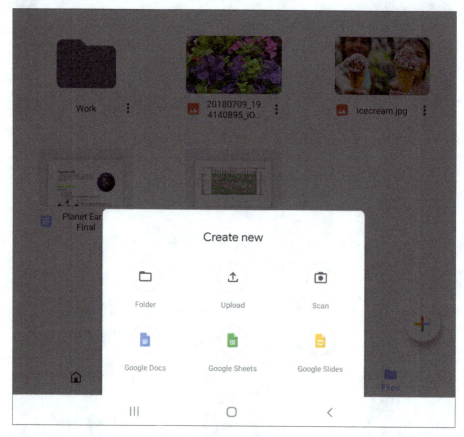

Along the bottom, you can create a new document, spreadsheet or slide presentation.

Scanning Documents

You can use the onboard camera to "scan" hard copy documents and convert them into PDFs.

First tap the '+' sign on the bottom right of the screen. Select 'scan' from the popup menu.

Now align the document, filling as much of the screen as possible. Make sure it's in focus.

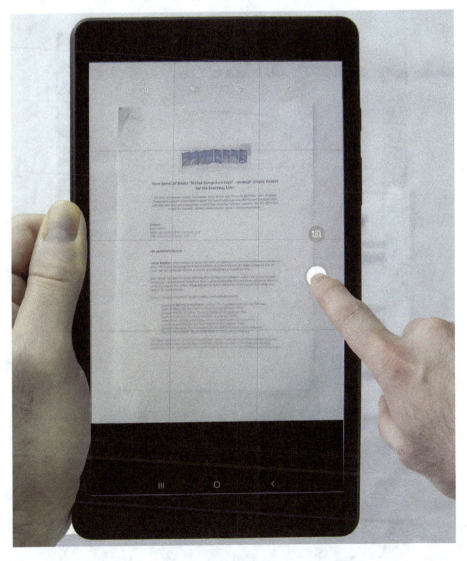

Tap the button at the bottom of the screen to "scan" the document.

You'll see the scan appear in the main window. Tap 'ok' if you're happy with the scan otherwise tap 'retry' and take the scan again.

Tap the '+' on the bottom left to add another page if the hard copy document has multiple pages, or tap the tick on the right hand side to finish.

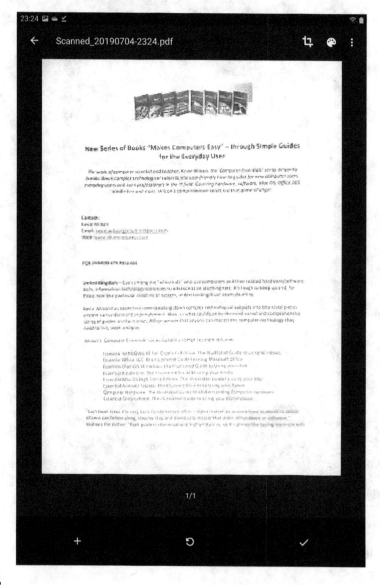

Enter a name for your document under 'document title' if needed.

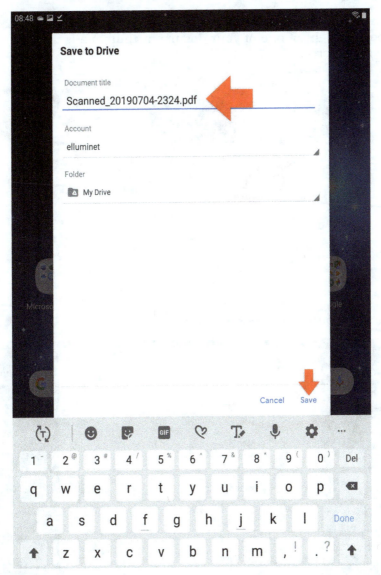

Tap 'save' on the bottom right of the screen. You might need to remove the onscreen keyboard if you can't see the 'save' button. Tap the down arrow on the bottom right to do this.

You'll find the scanned document appear as a PDF in your Google Drive documents.

Sharing Documents

To share a document with a friend or colleague, tap the 3 dots icon on the bottom right of one of your document thumbnails in your Google Drive main screen.

From the popup menu, select 'share'

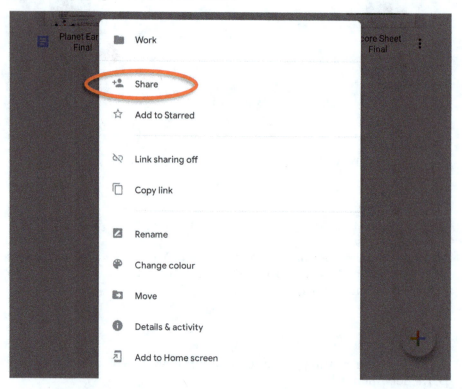

Enter the person's email address or name. You can add multiple addresses if there is more than one person.

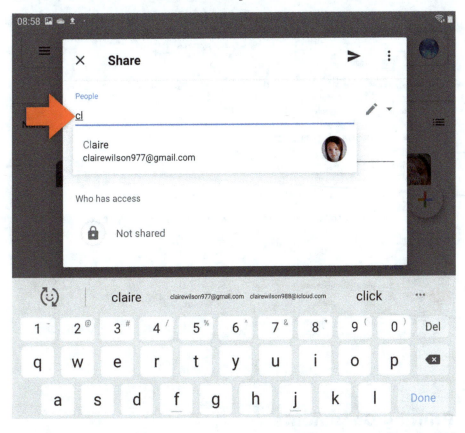

Now select what access you want to grant these people. You can select view only, or allow them to make changes to the document.

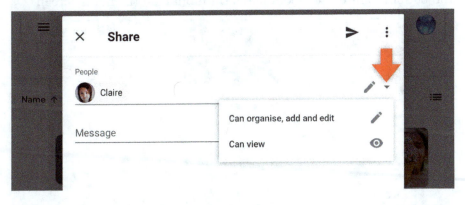

In this example, I'm going to allow Claire to edit the document, so I'm going to select 'can organise, add and edit'.

When the other person checks their email, they'll receive an invite to view the document. Just click/tap on the link.

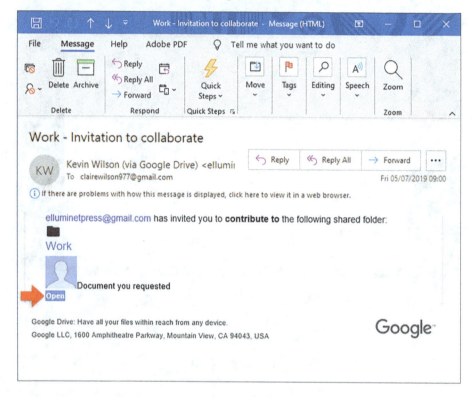

Printing Documents

To print a document from Google Drive, tap on the three dots icon on the bottom right of the document's thumbnail on the main screen.

Select 'print' from the popup menu.

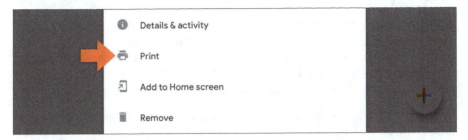

Select your printer from the options. If you don't see it, go set up your printer to use cloud printing in your printer's instructions.

On the top left you'll see 'copies', change this to the number of copies you want - leave it if you just want one copy. Change 'paper size' to the size of the paper: A4, letter, etc.

If you want to print specific pages, untick the ones you don't want using the tick box on the bottom right of each page preview.

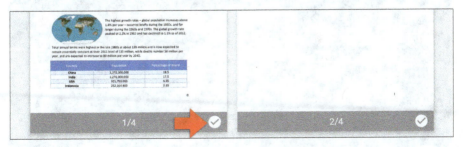

Tap the orange print icon on the top right to print your document

Google Maps

Google Maps is a web mapping service that offers satellite imagery, street maps, 360° panoramic street views, real-time traffic conditions, and directions for traveling by car, foot, or public transport. Google Maps can also be used as a GPS/SatNav on an android phone, giving turn-by-turn navigation while driving or walking.

To start the app, swipe downwards from the middle of the screen to reveal all your apps

Tap the 'Google' folder, then tap 'Maps'.

Map Type

You can change the map type, meaning you can change between road map, satellite map and terrain map. To do this, tap the icon on the top right.

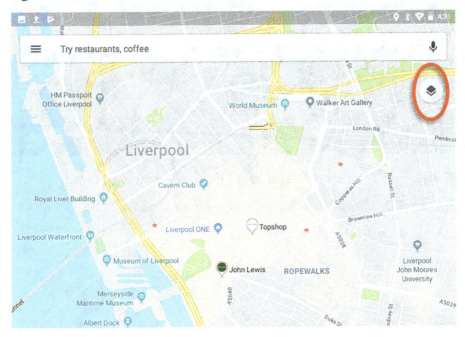

Select 'satellite' to view the satellite map.

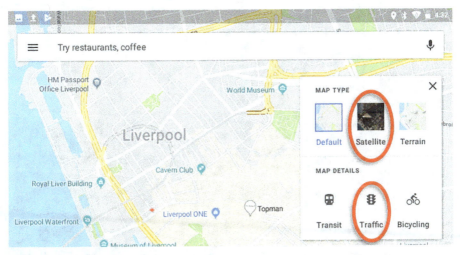

You can also add map details such as transit stats for public transport, and traffic stats for roads.

Exploring Maps & Getting Directions

In the field at the top of the screen, type in a postcode/zipcode, address or name of the place you want to get to.

Google maps will start to search for places matching your entry.

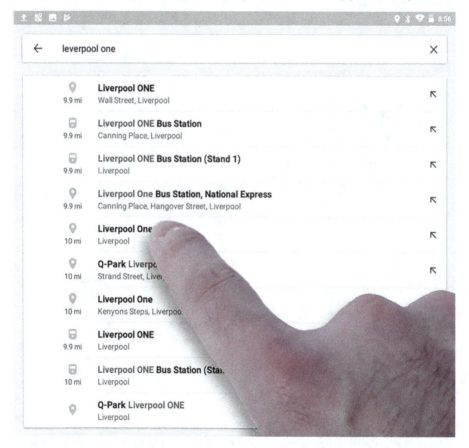

Tap on the one that matches.

You can move around the map using your finger. Tap and drag your finger across the glass.

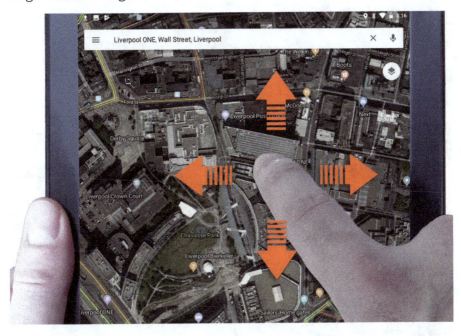

To zoom in and out, pinch the screen with your forefinger and thumb.

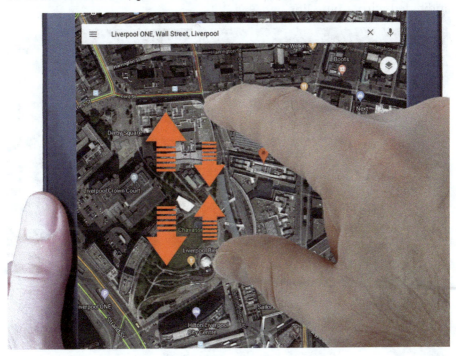

To get directions from your current position, tap 'directions'

Along the top you'll see your location and your destination. You can change either of these - just tap in the field and type in a new address.

Underneath you'll see an estimated travel time, for travelling by car, bus, walk or bike. The double arrow on the right hand side swaps your location and destination - useful to find your way back after you've been somewhere as it just reverses the route.

In the centre of the screen you'll see your route mapped out for you, indicated with a blue line.

Use your finger to move the map around to see your route. Use your forefinger and thumb to zoom in and out as before to take a close look at the parts of your route.

At the bottom, tap 'start' to begin navigation.

This acts like a GPS/Satnav and will give you turn by turn navigation as your drive.

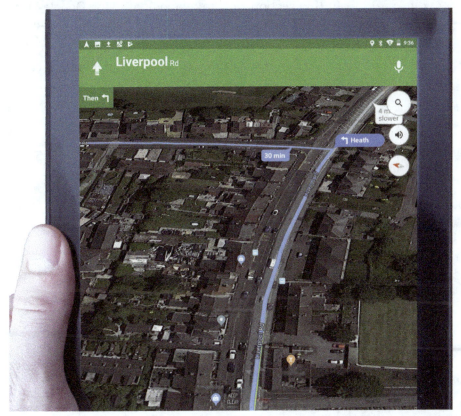

Using Google Docs

Google Docs is Google's online version of a word processor and works in a similar way to a cut down version of Microsoft Word.

In this section we'll take a look at using Google Docs to create simple every day documents with formatted text, images and tables.

Lets begin by installing Google Docs if it isn't already.

Installing Google Docs

If Google Docs is not already installed on your tablet, you'll need to download it from the Play Store. To do this, open the Play Store and search for Google Docs.

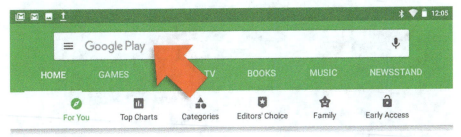

Tap 'install' on the right hand side.

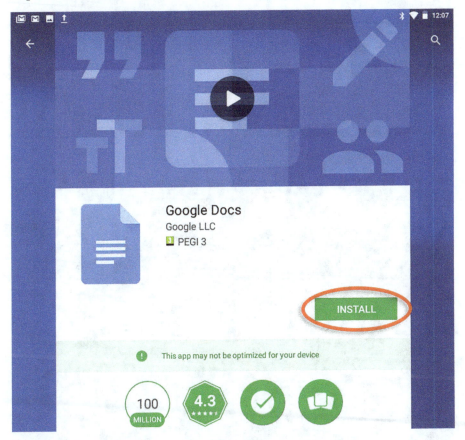

You'll find the Google Docs icon on your homescreen or in your app drawer..

Starting Google Docs

To start the Google Docs app, swipe downwards from the middle of the screen to reveal all your apps

Tap the 'docs' icon.

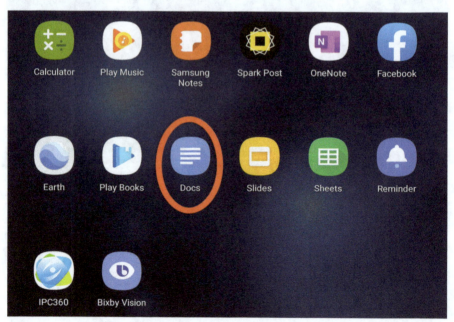

Google Docs will open. On the initial screen, you'll see preview thumbnails of the most recent documents you've edited or viewed. You can tap on any of these to resume your work.

To create a new document, tap the orange '+' icon on the bottom right. In this example, we'll be starting with a blank document.

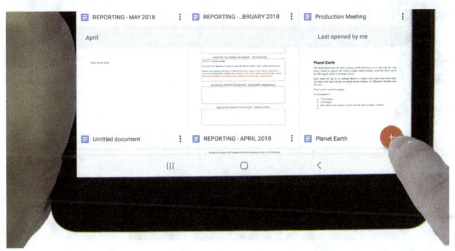

From the little popup menu that appears, select 'new document'.

Chapter 7: Using Google Docs

You can either use Google Docs in portrait mode. This mode is good for reading documents as you can see more of the page, and scroll up and down more easily.

Here you can see the full page more clearly for reading.

You can also use Google Docs in landscape mode - to do this, just rotate your tablet, the screen will automatically rotate the correct way around. This mode is better for typing and creating documents, as the onscreen keyboard is bigger and wider making it easier to type.

With the Galaxy S4, you can attach the external keyboard and use the tablet like a laptop.

Along the top you'll see the toolbar. This is where you'll find most of the tools you'll need to create and format your documents.

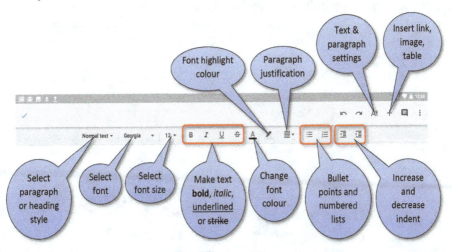

Using Paragraph Styles

Google Docs has several paragraph styles that are useful for keeping your formatting consistent.

For example you can set a font style, size and colour for a heading or title style...

Headings

To set the styles for a heading or paragraph, just highlight it with your mouse and click the drop down box 'normal text'.

To highlight the text, tap on the first word and hold your finger for a second, then drag your finger across the words.

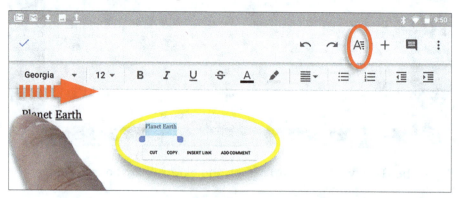

Once you've highlighted the words, tap the text and paragraphs icon on the top right. Select the 'text' panel if not already selected, go down to 'style' and change it to a heading style, eg, 'heading 1'.

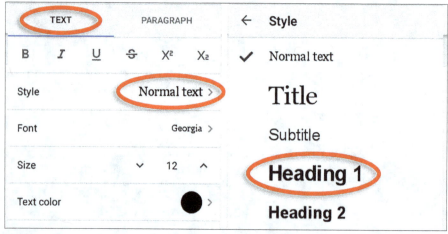

Bold, Italic, Underlined

To make text **bold**, *italic,* or <u>underlined</u>, highlight the text with your finger, then select the bold, italic, or underline icon from the toolbar.

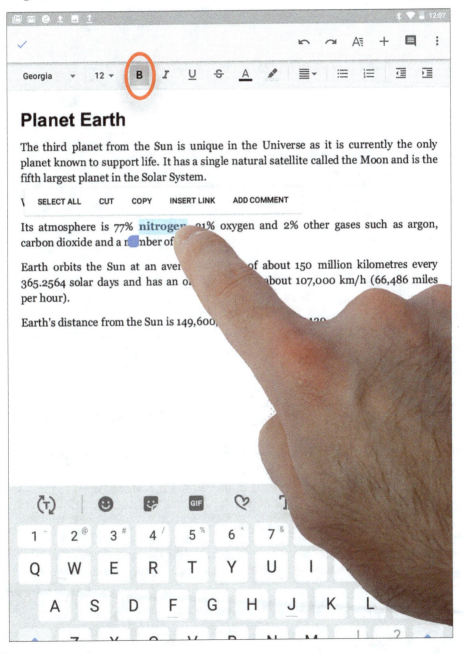

You can do the same for *italic,* <u>underlined</u> or ~~strikethrough~~ text.

Changing Fonts

Google Docs has a variety of fonts to choose from. To apply a different font to your text, highlight the text with your finger.

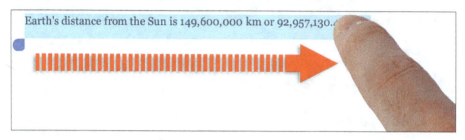

Tap the font style drop down box as shown below.

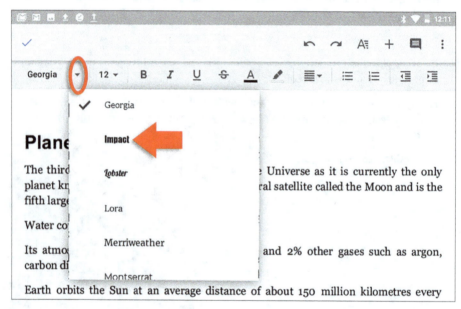

Select a font. You'll see the font change on your highlighted text.

Its atmosphere is 77% **nitrogen**, 21% oxygen and 2% other gases such as argon, carbon dioxide and a number of others.

Earth orbits the Sun at an average distance of about 150 million kilometres every 365.2564 solar days and has an orbital speed of about 107,000 km/h (66,486 miles per hour).

Earth's distance from the Sun is 149,600,000 km or 92,957,130.4 miles.

Font Colour

To change the colour of the text, first highlight it with your finger. In the example below, I want to change the text colour of the second paragraph.

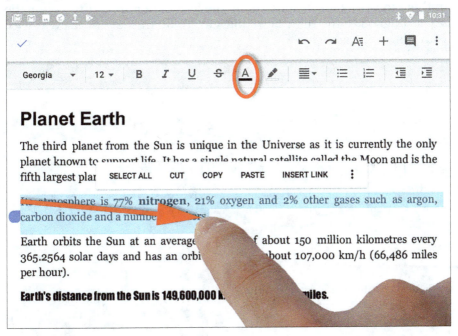

From the toolbar, select the font colour icon and from the drop down choose a colour. In this example I'm using red.

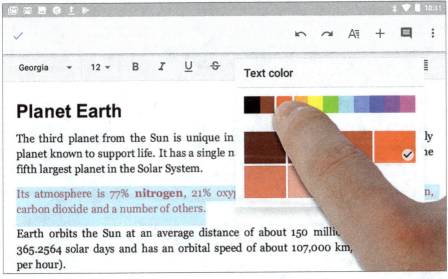

Justify Text

You can align text to different margins: Left, Centred, Right, Full. To do this, select the text you want to apply formatting to.

In this example, I want right justify the first paragraph. This means the text is aligned to the right hand margin. To do this, select the text with your finger to highlight it.

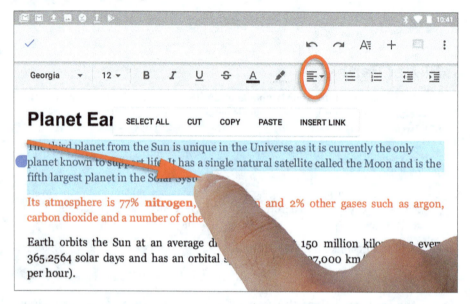

Select the right align icon from the toolbar.

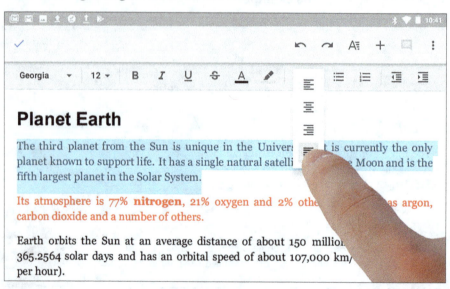

Bullets and Numbered Lists

Select the text using your finger as shown below.

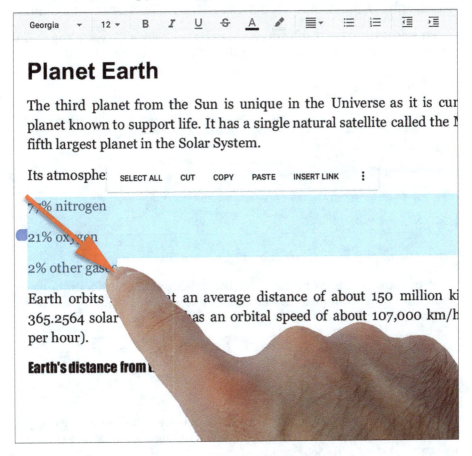

Then from the toolbar, click the bullet points icon.

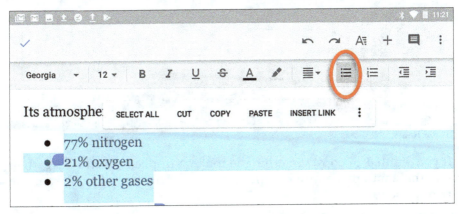

Cut, Copy & Paste

To ease editing documents, you can use copy, cut, and paste to move paragraphs or pictures around on different parts of your document.

First, select the paragraph you want to cut or copy with your finger. I'm going to cut the last paragraph in the document below.

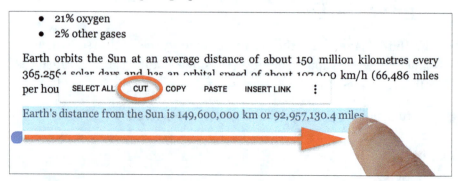

From the popup menu, select 'cut'. Insert a blank line.

Now tap and hold your finger on the position in the document you want the paragraph you just cut out to be inserted. Tap 'paste' when it appears.

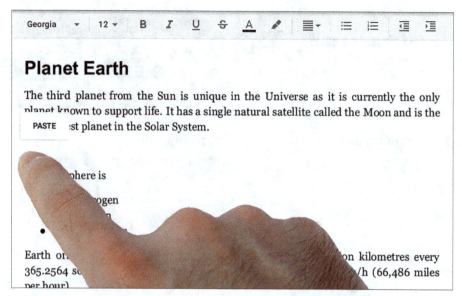

If you wanted to copy something ie make a duplicate of the text, then use the same procedure except select 'copy' instead of 'cut' from the popup menu.

Adding Images

You can insert images from your camera, google photos and the web.

To insert an image, tap the '+' icon on the top right of your toolbar

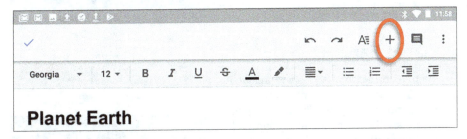

From the drop down menu, select where you want to add your image from: photos stored in your personal google photos, take one with your camera, or search for one on the web. In this example, I'm going to insert an image from the web.

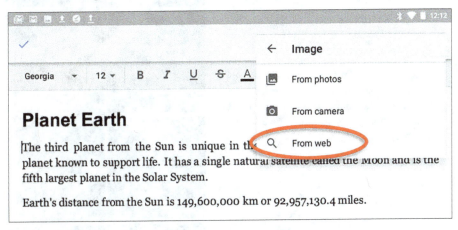

Type your search into the search bar on the top right.

I'm looking for photos of the earth, so I'd type in 'earth'. Change this to whatever you're looking for.

From the search results, tap on the image you want to add.

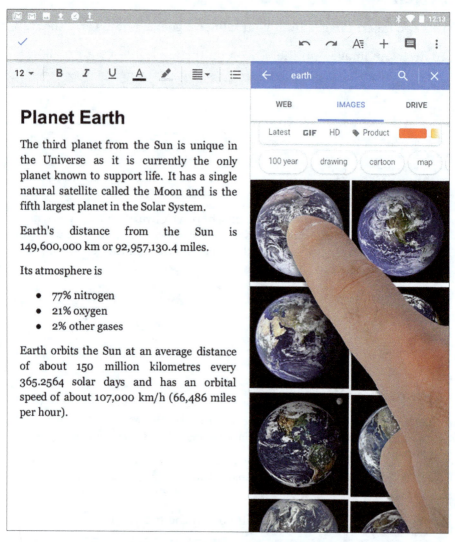

Tap 'insert' on the top right.

You'll need to resize your image and adjust the text wrapping to make it fit into your document

Resize Images

You can change the size of your image if it is too small or too large. To do this, tap on the image. You'll see eight blue squares around the edge of the image. These are called resize handles.

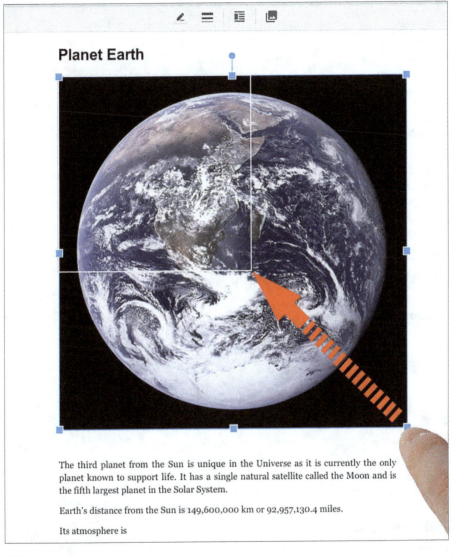

Tap and drag the corner resize handle inwards to make the image smaller.

Whenever possible, use the corners to resize the image. This helps to keep the image from being squashed or distorted when resizing.

Adding Tables

To add a table, tap on the position in your document you want the table to appear, then tap on the '+' icon on the top right of the screen.

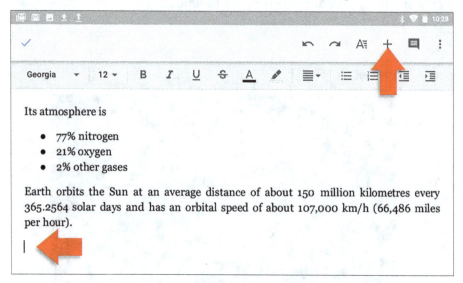

From the drop down 'insert' menu, select 'table'.

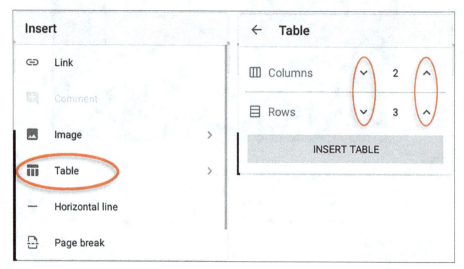

Then on the 'table' menu, select how many rows and columns you want using the up & down arrows.

Tap 'insert table' when you're done.

You can type into each cell in the table as normal

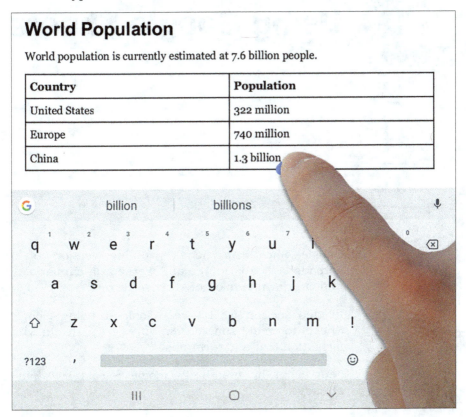

Enter any text using the on screen keyboard.

Using Google Sheets

Google Sheets is Google's online version of a spreadsheet programme and works in a similar way to a cut down version of Microsoft Excel.

In this section we'll take a look at using Google Sheets to create simple every day spreadsheets with formatted text and formulas.

Lets begin by installing Google Sheets if it isn't already.

Installing Google Sheets

If google sheets is not already installed on your tablet, you'll need to download it from the play store. To do this, open the play store and search for google sheets.

Tap 'install' on the right hand side.

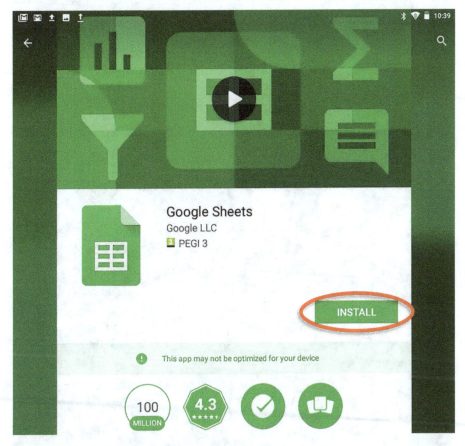

You'll find the google sheets icon on your homescreen or in your app drawer..

215

Starting Google Sheets

To start the Google Docs app, swipe downwards from the middle of the screen to reveal all your apps

Tap the 'sheets' icon.

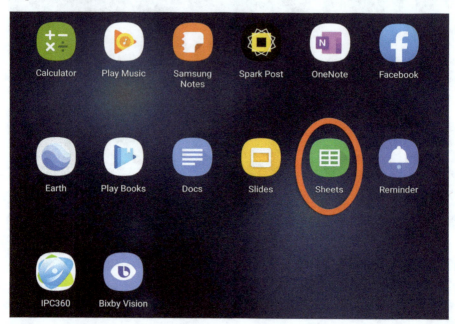

Google Sheets will open. On the initial screen, you'll see preview thumbnails of the most recent spreadsheets you've edited or viewed. You can tap on any of these to resume your work.

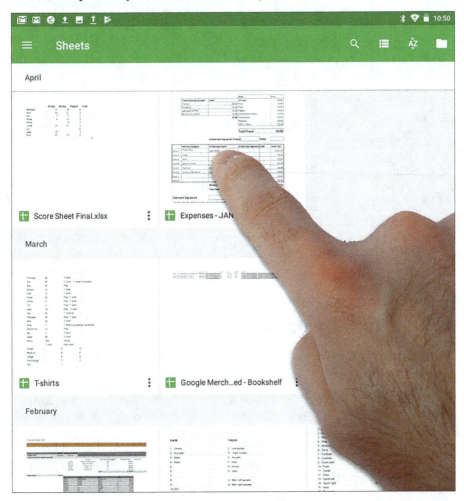

To create a new spreadsheet, tap the orange '+' icon on the bottom right. In this example, we'll be starting with a blank document.

From the little popup menu that appears, select 'new spreadsheet'.

Entering Data

In this example we are doing a basic scoring sheet.

Simple Text Formatting

Sometimes it improves the readability of your spreadsheet to format the data in the cells.

First you need to select the cells you want to format. In this example, I want to select the dates and total along the top of the spreadsheet above. To do this, tap on the first cell - you'll see a blue border appear with two dots either side.

Tap and drag the dot across the cells you want to select.

218

Inserting Rows & Columns

You can insert rows and columns in your spreadsheet using the buttons on the toolbar at the top of the screen

Insert a Row

To insert a row, tap and select the row in your spreadsheet where you want to insert a blank row. In this example, I want to add a row between 'Joan' and 'Eva'.

		22-Apr	29-Apr	Played	Total	
1						
2	Barbara	21	19	2		
3	Ann	10	21	2		
4	Flo	7	7	2		
5	Rose	9	12	2		
6	Emily		0	1		
7	Josie	21	21	2		
8	Lin			0		
9	Joan	19		1		
	Eva	21	14	2		

Select the 'insert row after' icon, on the top right of your screen.

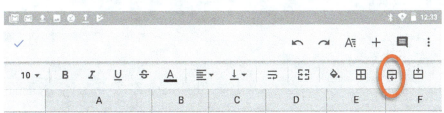

You'll see a blank row appear

9	Joan	19		1	
10					
11	Eva	21	14	2	

219

Insert a Column

To insert a column, tap and select the column in your spreadsheet where you want to insert a blank column. In this example, I want to add a row between the last date and the 'total'.

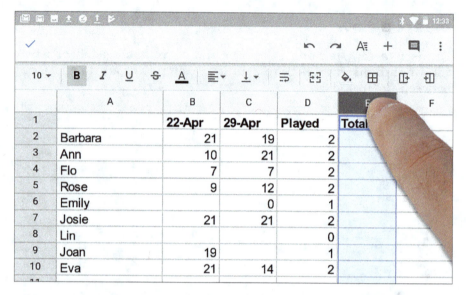

Select the 'insert column after' icon, on the top right of your screen.

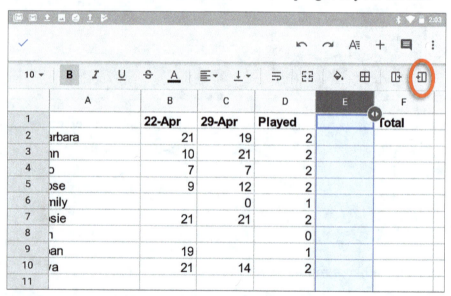

You'll see a blank column appear

Cell Borders

To add borders, first you need to select the cells you want to format. In this example, I want to select the names. To do this, tap on the first cell - you'll see a blue border appear with two dots either side. Drag the dot on the bottom right down over the names as shown below.

		22-Apr	29-Apr	Played	Total	
1						
2	Barbara	21	19	2	42	
3	Ann	10	21	2		
4	Flo	7	7	2		
5	Rose	9	12	2		
6	Emily		0	1		
7	Josie	21	21	2		
8	Lin			0		
9	Joan	19		1		
10	Eva	21	14	2		
11						
12						
13						
14						
15						
16						
17						
18						

From the toolbar, select the borders icon.

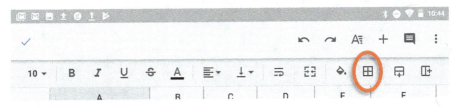

From the dialog box, select border type, style and colour.

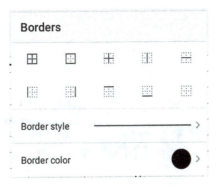

Cell Shading

To add shading to the cells, first you need to select the cells you want to format. In this example, I want to select the names. To do this, tap on the first cell - you'll see a blue border appear with two dots either side. Drag the dot on the bottom right down over the names as shown below.

		22-Apr	29-Apr	Played	Total		
1							
2	Barbara	21	19	2	42		
3	Ann	10	21	2			
4	Flo	7	7	2			
5	Rose	9	12	2			
6	Emily		0	1			
7	Josie	21	21	2			
8	Lin			0			
9	Joan	19		1			
10	Eva	21	14	2			
11							
12							
13							
14							
15							
16							
17							
18							

Select the shading icon from the toolbar.

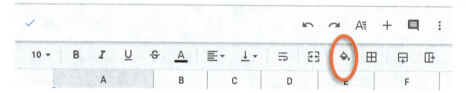

From the dialog box, select a colour from the pallet.

Using Functions

You'll find the functions bar at the bottom of your screen when you tap inside a cell.

	A	B	C	D	E	F
1		22-Apr	29-Apr	Played	Total	
2	Barbara	21	19	2		
3	Ann	10	21	2		
4	Flo	7	7	2		
5	Rose	9	12	2		
6	Emily		0	1		
7	Josie	21	21	2		
8	Lin			0		
9	Joan	19		1		
10	Eva	21	14	2		
11						
12						
13						

fx Enter text or formula

I want to add up the scores for the two dates (B2 & C2) in the spreadsheet above.

In the 'enter text or formula' bar at the bottom. First enter an = sign. This tells google sheets to expect a formula or function.

fx =

Now type in the name of the function. Since we want to add the numbers up, type...

    SUM (

To find other functions, tap the 'fx' icon on the left hand side and select the function you want.

223

Now, tap on the first number in the series to be added together. In this example it's cell B2 containing the number 21.

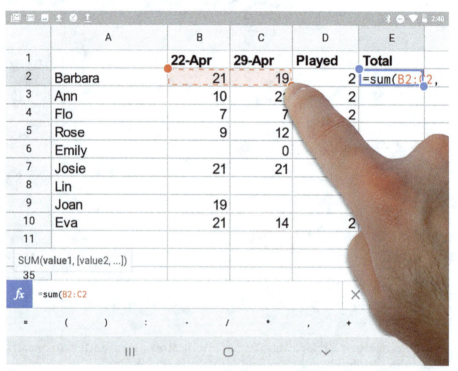

Now drag the red dot across the rest of the numbers.

In the 'fx' formula bar along the bottom, make sure the formula is correct.

Sometimes google sheets adds extra punctuation marks such as comas - remove these, so you just have your function. Close your bracket.

Tap the green 'enter' button on your on screen keyboard.

In this example, you should end up with...

=sum(B2:C2)

Copy the function or formula to the rest of the column

To do this, tap on the cell you added the function to. Drag the blue dot down the rest of the column.

Tap and hold your finger on the selected cells, until you see a popup menu.

Select 'autofill' from the menu.

# Video Resources

To help you understand the procedures and concepts explored in this book, we have developed some video resources and app demos for you to use, as you work through the book.

To find the resources, open your web browser and navigate to the following website

`www.elluminetpress.com/taba`

At the beginning of each chapter, you'll find a website that contains the resources for that chapter.

When you open the link to the video resources, you'll see a thumbnail list at the bottom.

Click on the thumbnail for the particular video you want to watch. Most videos are between 30 and 60 seconds outlining the procedure, others are a bit longer.

When the video is playing, hover your mouse over the video and you'll see some controls...

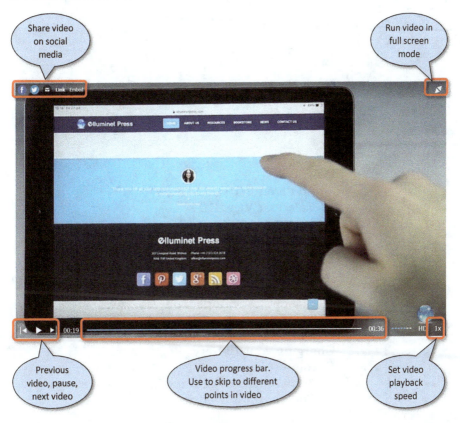

Index

Index

Index

N

O

P

S

T

U

Upgrading Android 20

V

Video Chat 107
VPN 54

W

Wallpaper 41
Web Browser 77
WiFi 52

Z

Zoom in/out 63